THROUGH A MOTHER'S TEARS

*The tragic true story of a mother who lost
one daughter to a brutal murderer and another to
a broken heart*

CATHY BROOMFIELD

THISTLE
PUBLISHING

This first edition published in 2018 by:

Thistle Publishing
36 Great Smith Street
London
SW1P 3BU

www.thistlepublishing.co.uk

To the memory of my darling daughters, Kirsty and Hayley, whose short stay on this earth made a lasting impression on so many people's hearts and minds.

ACKNOWLEDGMENTS

I would like to thank my husband Dave - my gentle giant and soulmate. Without you I doubt that I would still be here. Thank you for standing by me through all the tragedies we have had to overcome. Also my precious daughter Sonya who has been such a wonderful support, my beautiful grandchildren and my sisters who were there when it mattered and when I needed them. I love you all very much.

Thank you from the bottom of my heart to Bernadette Thompson for helping me, with kindness and patience, to write my story, and many thanks to Caro Handley for believing in it and to Andrew Lownie and Thistle Publishing for putting it into print.

PROLOGUE
THE ANNOUNCEMENT

January 2008

The evening that Kirsty rang to tell us her big news, Dave and I were curled up watching television. We had just got back from a Christmas Holiday in Turkey; it was cold and dark outside, but Kirsty brightened my spirits as soon as I heard her giggling down the phone.

'Guess what, Mum? I'm getting married.' I could hear the happiness and excitement in her voice.

'Married? Kirsty, that's fantastic. You and Jonny make a lovely couple.' I was delighted and I felt a rush of pleasure. Kirsty had been seeing Jonny for over two years and she thought the world of him. We did too, he was a lovely bloke. I was so happy for them.

'No Mum. It's not Jonny I'm marrying. I've met somebody called Paul and we're getting married.'

'What do you mean you've met somebody called Paul and you're getting married?'

'We're getting married in five weeks. We've already set a date.'

'Hang on a minute, we don't even know him. Where did you meet him?'

'I went to a party and he was there. We'd had a one night stand ages ago, and I sort of recognised him, and he recognised me. And it clicked we'd met each other before.' She giggled, 'You know my friend Vicky? It turns out he's her brother. Mum, he's the one – my soul mate, the man of my dreams. I'll bring him to meet you in a couple of days. You'll just love him, I know you will.'

I was trying to take in what she was telling me. 'But Kirsty, you've only known him for two minutes. And what about Jonny? What's the big rush to get married to this Paul?'

'I've finished with Jonny, forget about him. Me and Paul have already set the date, February 16th. Look I've got to go. We'll come over in a couple of days and you can meet him. Alright? Bye Mum, love to Dave.' Then she was gone; I was left holding the phone, as a feeling of absolute dread ran through my whole body.

CHAPTER ONE
BEFORE

It was no secret that I had been married three times; when
we got married my first husband, John, was seventeen and
I was eighteen, far too young, and I was pregnant within
months. Even before my beautiful Sonya was born, cracks
had already started to show in the marriage. John was out
nearly every night, gambling and sleeping with other women.
I left him when Sonya was two, and although it was a struggle
we managed alone for about 6 years and were very happy.

My second husband, Fred, was the father of my two
younger daughters, Hayley and Kirsty. Actually, Fred and I
never married but were 'Common Law' husband and wife,
living together and giving the impression that we were married, which felt important at the time.

When Hayley was born I thought she was so gorgeous;
I couldn't believe that she was all mine, she was so perfect
and I was over the moon. From day one Hayley was a 'good'
baby, she never woke for feeds, slept through the night,
and was a contented and incredibly intelligent child. When
she was fifteen months old and I was heavily pregnant with
Kirsty we had a family holiday at Butlin's in Skegness. To
my delight, she came first in the Bonny Baby Competition.
I still have the certificate and the teddy bear that she won.

When Kirsty Leanne arrived, I couldn't believe my luck – another beautiful baby. After she was born I sat up in the hospital bed, cradling her in my arms; I was laughing and crying at the same time, and I kept repeating 'Oh my God, I don't believe it, it's a girl – it's a girl!' I was absolutely over the moon and the midwife and nurses smiled at me and asked if it was my first daughter. 'No!' I giggled. 'She's my third. But I wanted another girl so much, and here she is.' As I gazed down at that tiny face I really felt as if I'd won the lottery; on that day all of my dreams were fulfilled.

We all immediately fell in love with her, Hayley most of all; she enjoyed helping me feed and bathe the new baby, and despite being as different as chalk and cheese the two girls grew very close. Hayley was very quiet and thoughtful, taking pleasure in keeping her things nice, whereas Kirsty was lively and outgoing and managed to break or wreck her belongings. We used to laugh and say that one was constructive and the other was destructive!

I used to dress them the same and people often took them for twins, even though Kirsty was much smaller than Hayley. They shared a real bond, as close, I think, as actual twins. When Kirsty started trying to speak Hayley often had to interpret for me as I didn't understand what she was saying. They were still pretty young when Hayley began calling Kirsty 'Stig', from Stig of the Dump, because her hair was always wild and messy. In return Kirsty began calling Hayley 'Ginge', because of her reddish hair colour. In the beginning, they called each other those names just to be annoying, but eventually the names stuck and that's what they called each other for the rest of their lives.

My relationship with Fred didn't last; he never hit me, not once, but he tortured me mentally, day after day, and that can be almost worse than any other form of abuse. In

1985 I remember people talking about the Band Aid concerts, when Bob Geldof raised millions of pounds for famine relief, and I remember seeing, because it frightened me, the Broadwater Farm Riots in Tottenham on the news, and the resulting tragedy of PC Keith Blakelock being stabbed, but none of it really touched me. I was too concerned with caring for my babies and trying to protect myself from Fred. I asked him to leave when Kirsty was only three months old and Hayley nineteen months old and, to my relief, he moved out straight away.

We didn't see or hear from Fred again for about twelve years, and then suddenly he started phoning me and being really nasty, making threats towards me and the girls, telling me what he would do to me and his 'beloved' daughters, Hayley and Kirsty. He rang night after night after night. It was horrible, he was sick in the head, and I got so frightened he would come after us that I took the girls to a woman's refuge. We lived there for five months before we were finally offered a house in Redditch and we were delighted. I just wanted to live quietly with my girls, without a man around to cheat, gamble, or mentally abuse me.

I think that my parents' divorce so many years before, when I was nine years old, had affected my three sisters and me very badly. We were shoved from pillar to post. We lived first with an aunt, and then with my Granny in Scotland, and then my mum moved us into a two-roomed flat. About two years after they split up, my dad suddenly turned up out of the blue, and it was during his visit that I realised how much I missed him. I was a real daddy's girl and I begged to go and live with him. I was only 13 and at first they said no, but I cried and cried until they gave in and said I could go back to Coventry with him. But my stepmother, who had two younger children of her own with my father, was very jealous of my relationship with him and that caused a lot of friction. Mum married a lovely man when I was fifteen and I was really happy for her. Soon afterwards she moved back to Coventry and as I was missing my sisters and my stepmother was making my life miserable, I went back to live with Mum. A few years later Dad left his second wife and then got together with a woman who was younger than me and had another son, my younger brother Danny. After my dad left my mum, I found it hard to trust men and my first two marriages only deepened those feelings. So when the local council in Redditch offered us the house it was like a dream come true.

The house was in a terrible state; it was filthy and badly in need of decorating. In fact, one of the bedrooms had black gloss paint handprints on the ceiling. Who on earth had lived there before, and what sort of people were they? But I didn't care. It was ours. I would clean and decorate and make it into a comfortable home for the three of us. I rolled up my sleeves and got to work.

The women's refuge had offered me the choice of a house in Redditch or a house in Droitwich, and I had chosen the former. Later in my life I would often think about the film 'Sliding Doors' and wonder if my girls would still be alive today if I had chosen to go to the house in Droitwich instead. I will never know.

Hayley was a really clever little girl, and at 11 years old she took an exam to get a scholarship to Bablake Grammar School in Coventry. She passed with flying colours, as we knew she would, and we were so proud of her that the whole family went out for a meal to celebrate.

She was also a very unique individual, preferring her own style to following the latest fashion trends; she always said she didn't want to be a sheep and follow everyone else.

4

At the age of twelve, she painted her fingernails black, wore deep purple lipstick, and declared herself a 'Goth'. I wasn't even sure what that was! The next thing she was wearing tie-dye blouses and floaty skirts, and playing the guitar that she'd begged me to buy her, and which she quickly learned to play on her own without lessons. My dad was a first-class guitar player and could play any musical instrument by ear, and Hayley took after him in that respect. She loved music, listening to it and playing it at any opportunity.

At one time Hayley decided she was going to be a vegetarian. I tried my hardest to cook tasty vegetarian meals for her but the internet wasn't readily available then and I couldn't just look up recipes online. What a headache. But I did laugh when, with me going doolally everyday trying to cook appetising meals for her, I found out that she was getting up in the middle of the night and eating all the cold meat in the fridge. I thought I was going mad when the food kept disappearing! Needless to say, her vegetarianism didn't last long.

Sonya was working in a job centre when she met John; he worked in a factory and although he was more than twenty years older than her he treated her as if she was a princess. I had no concerns about their relationship at all and was delighted when they got married. The wedding was at about the same time I met Dave, who was to become my third husband, and I wasn't even looking for a relationship at the time.

The funny thing was, Kirsty already knew Dave. Across the road from where we lived in Redditch was a family club that Kirsty and her friends used to go to, to practice their Spice Girl routines on the stage. Back then 12 year-old Kirsty was mad about the Spice Girls. Dave sometimes used to treat the girls to free bottles of pop and packets of crisps if they didn't have any money. Dave's sister Penny and brother in law Rod were the managers of the club, and Dave used to drink in there, but sometimes he helped out behind the bar. He was a roofer and I was a stay at home Mom. Kirsty told him that I didn't have a boyfriend and that he would like me if he met me, and she was right.

This was 1997, the year Channel Five began broadcasting, which meant we were suddenly spoilt for choice with the five TV channels; we couldn't afford to have Sky or cable back then, just normal television. The girls and I loved watching the Eurovision Song Contest; we used to make it a special night with snacks and fizzy drinks for the girls, and the UK actually won that year, which is why I remember it. For some reason, Dolly the Sheep sticks in my mind then too; I remember the girls laughing and joking about Dolly the Sheep, they thought its name was so funny, and there was an advert on the radio about two sheep arguing about which one was the real Dolly. The biggest news of the year though, was the tragic death of Princess Diana and Dodi Fayed in a Paris car crash. I remember being glued to the television the whole of that Sunday after we heard the news, and on the day of her funeral I just couldn't stop watching the television and crying. It was all so sad.

One night my next-door neighbour invited me to the club for a game of bingo, and we stayed afterwards for a drink. I hardly ever went there but it was my 42nd birthday and I thought 'why not?'. Dave was in the club as well and he bought me a few birthday drinks; being a typical bloke, he didn't say much to me – but he did tell some of the other blokes in the club that he fancied me. They had a good belly laugh at that and told him he had no chance of getting off with me, so he bet them ten pounds that he could, even though he was very shy. Well, he won the bet and we started going out together.

Kirsty had slept in my bed with me for years, so when Dave started to stay over there was a little bit of jealousy and resentment, but it only lasted for about half an hour. That's how Kirsty was, she could have a massive argument with you and about two seconds later it was all forgotten. Dave got on great with my girls and, not having seen or heard from Fred for about twelve years, they quickly started looking upon Dave as their dad, and he was happy to be their adopted father. He was a kind and loving man, and would do anything for us. He was known locally as the gentle giant because he is so tall, 6ft 8 inches tall to my 5ft 1, and a lot of people stared because of the height difference but we have never let it bother us.

When we met, Dave had been married for nearly twenty years and he had two grown up children, David and Michelle. His wife had had an affair with a married man and after a short time the two of them went off together. Coincidentally, the married man and his wife had been living just three doors down from where I lived at the time. So when Dave and I got together we decided it would be good to move away and make a fresh start with Kirsty and Hayley, just the four of us.

CHAPTER TWO
THE FATAL MOVE

1998

We were put in touch with a young couple in South Wales who wanted to move to the Midlands, so one weekend we went to have a look at their house and the area to see what we thought. We all fell for the house; it had a front room and dining room, with a good-sized kitchen at the back, while upstairs were three bedrooms and bathroom, and the back garden was lovely. I could picture Dave and myself sitting out there in the summer with a cold drink, and I knew we could be happy there. It was a small road in a quiet area and that suited us just fine, so we exchanged houses and moved in as soon as we could. It was less than a year after Dave and I had met.

When we moved to Bridgend Sonya and John stayed in Coventry, but we were in touch constantly, and Hayley and Kirsty grew even closer since they'd left all their friends behind. At 13 and 14 they were still more like twins than sisters.

For some reason, Kirsty hated being on her own in the house; it frightened her so much that she couldn't even look at Crimewatch if she was by herself. She was a gentle and loving girl who absolutely adored animals; if she found any creature that was injured or abandoned she would rescue the poor thing and bring it home. She often gave to children's charities despite having little money of her own, and would never speak ill of anyone, only seeing the good in other people. She really was a gentle girl, and everyone who met her loved her.

I used to call Kirsty my 'pink princess' because she loved the colour pink, and she dreamed about all the things she imagined a fairy-tale princess had: big hair, carriages, ball gowns, a prince charming! She loved clothes and fashion, and was forever poring over celebrity magazines to see what the latest stars were wearing, and daydreaming about having everything pink and girly and celebrity that was in the Littlewoods catalogue.

My pink princess was a very pretty blonde and had always been tiny; she weighed under 5lb at birth and was still only six stone. She wanted to be a model 'like Jordan', who she idolised, and it helped that she had a presence that brightened a room as soon as she walked in. I'd often find her posing in front of the mirror in various outfits, or practicing her make-up. I had no doubt that, if it's what she wanted, she could be a model one day as she definitely had the looks and personality for it.

I was so proud of all of my girls; I couldn't have been more delighted that Sonya was happy and settled with John in the Midlands. Hayley and Kirsty were real friends and supported each other in whatever they did, whether it was getting up to a bit of mischief, or needing a shoulder to cry on. They even went together to get tattoos inked onto their wrists; they each had a little star, and used to joke that they were 'sistars'.

Hayley was only seventeen when she met a boy named John and moved to Wrexham with him, a hundred and fifty miles away. Kirsty was, for the first time, living at home with just Dave and me. She moped around for a while but she soon started going out with friends more, and she and Hayley texted every day.

Three months later Hayley found out she was pregnant. I was talking to her on the phone one night and she was bemoaning the fact that she didn't have a washing machine and had piles of washing to do, so I told her to find the nearest launderette. That's what we all did before everyone had a washing machine in the house.

I've already mentioned that the girls took to Dave straight away and, apart from being the shy quiet type, he was a kind and giving person. While I was on the phone with Hayley telling her to find a launderette, Dave had the Argos catalogue out and was ordering her a brand-new washing machine. That's the sort of man he is, and he could never bear to see the girls going without.

When Hayley's daughter Megan Eve was born, Dave and I went straight up to see our new grandchild. She was beautiful and I wished they lived closer so I could see more of her. Hayley and John had an extremely volatile relationship, always arguing and fighting, and being so alone, so far away from the family, and with a little baby to care for, Hayley couldn't cope; she was just too young and inexperienced.

John and Hayley split up and John's parents, Sue and Eric, took Megan Eve to live with them in Chester where they were managing a golf club. Hayley escaped to Bristol to try to rebuild her life, and soon after that she moved to Northampton, and then to London, but she couldn't settle; she tried coming home to South Wales for a while, but that didn't work either, and she finally ended up back in the Midlands where she felt more at home.

Around the same time, in 2001, Dave was rushed to hospital with chest pains; he was seriously ill and I was so scared for him, and for me. I didn't want to lose him. The doctors thought he wasn't going to make it through the night, and I was advised to call his family to let them know how ill he was and for them to come and say their last goodbyes. His family were in total shock. They travelled from the Midlands to South Wales to see him, but after a mechanical valve was put in place in his aorta, Dave pulled through. At the same time, they also discovered that he had Marfan Syndrome.

The doctors explained it to us. Marfan Syndrome is a disorder of the body's connective tissues – a group of tissues that maintain the structure of the body and support internal organs and other tissues. It leads to abnormal production of a protein called fibrillin, resulting in parts of the body being able to stretch abnormally when placed under any kind of stress; as well as all that, some bones tend to grow longer than they should. This means a person with Marfan Syndrome may be tall because their arms and legs grow longer than normal. It can lead to heart defects, and cause lens dislocation – where the lens of the eye falls into an abnormal position. Marfan Syndrome is also hereditary and can be life threatening.

It explained a lot; why Dave was so tall, and why he had always had trouble with his eyes, right from when he was a child – he'd had several operations on them. And now his heart problems. On top of everything else his eyes now deteriorated so rapidly that he had to stop work; he was taking an assortment of different medications, and I became his registered full time carer.

That same year the September 11th attack on the twin towers in New York was absolutely shocking and unbelievable, and watching it unfold on television was like watching a film. It was incredibly moving when, two days after the attacks, the Queen broke with tradition and ordered the Changing of the Guard ceremony to be paused for a two-minute silence, followed by the playing of The Star-Spangled Banner, in tribute to the victims of those dreadful attacks. I was glued to the television for days.

We had a few really happy years, despite Dave's illness and Hayley's ups and downs; Hayley settled in Coventry near Sonya, and I was pleased about that because she had her older sister close by and she seemed contented at last. Sonya and John made me a grandmother again with Anais and Amelia Rose. Kirsty moved to Swansea, she was beginning to break into glamour modelling and was very happy with her boyfriend Jonny. She really was living the dream. Dave had restored my faith in men after my two disastrous marriages, and if I ever mentioned that I was keen on something, he would do his best to get it for me. Life was good.

If I'd known then what I know now, I'd have packed the whole family up and moved them to the other side of the world to keep them safe and happy. But I couldn't have known that a nightmare was about to begin.

CHAPTER THREE
THE WEDDING

That January, 2008, was wet and windy, and we really felt the cold after our trip to Turkey. The local news was dominated by the closure of the Tower Colliery in South Wales; so many local people were associated with the coal mining industry in one way or another, and the mood was bleak.

Kirsty had rung to tell us that she was marrying Paul Grabham in a matter of weeks, and that didn't make things any better. She didn't know the first thing about Paul Grabham, and neither did we. Who was he? Where was he from? I felt sick just thinking about it but we knew we would have to tread carefully if we were to persuade Kirsty to slow down a bit, and we hoped that when we met him he would be a decent sort of bloke.

When Kirsty brought Paul home a couple of nights later, I couldn't believe what I was seeing. He was smelly, scruffy and unkempt, and he was full of piercings; his teeth were in such a bad way that when he laughed he sort of curled his top lip over them to hide how black and rotten they were. He had no job and he showed no evidence that he was in love with my daughter, or that he planned to care for or support her. In actual fact, Kirsty was making good money by this time, as a glamour model. She had her own flat, and this Paul had already moved in with her. As far as I could tell, Kirsty was supporting him.

Dave and I tried to be friendly and asked him what his job was; he said he was looking for work and he would find some soon enough because he was a trained plumber, a chef, a gas fitter, a male stripper, and a sports car racer. What? At the age of twenty-three? Did he think we were stupid? Talk about disillusioned!

Kirsty was wild with excitement and I tried to be happy for her and to hide my shock at the whole situation. I took her into the kitchen and asked her if she knew what she was doing, but she just said she loved him and wanted to be his wife. Both Dave and I advised them to wait a little longer before marrying but there was no talking to them, and they left shortly afterwards.

Dave and I were really worried; after meeting Paul Grabham we didn't trust him, didn't like him, and felt that something wasn't quite right about the whole set up. It was obvious that he was a parasite, but what could we do? From experience, we knew that the more we tried to talk Kirsty out of doing something, then the more determined she would be to go ahead with it.

Even so, I had such a bad feeling about Grabham that I begged Kirsty to wait just a few months before marrying Paul, even just until June, to get married, to get to know him a little bit better. I know she'd met him before but she hadn't known him for very long; Kirsty wasn't having any of it. She laughed off our fears; she was in love, he loved her, we were worrying for nothing, they would be fine. She was caught up in a whirlwind, making plans for the wedding and her future, and dreaming about which wedding dress she should have. We reluctantly gave her our support, even though the blood ran cold in my veins when I thought about Paul Grabham. Her happiness was all that mattered, and I could see that she really was happy.

Sonya confided in me that she hadn't taken to Paul at all and felt he was too much of a Jack the Lad; she couldn't see what on earth Kirsty saw in him. She couldn't understand how her beautiful younger sister had got mixed up with such a lowlife and had her heart set on spending the rest of her life with him. Hayley had similar feelings and had tried to talk Kirsty out of marrying him as well, but she wouldn't listen to any of us.

Dave and I took Kirsty shopping in Swansea for a wedding dress. She was bubbling with excitement at all the lace and tulle, silk and satin, ribbons and sparkles, tiaras and shoes. She absolutely loved it and she tried on dozens of dresses until she found the right one. It was an exhausting but fantastic day, she was my pink princess again and despite my reservations about her choice of groom, it gave me such pleasure to see her so excited and happy.

Kirsty stayed with us for the ten nights leading up to the wedding, and we were all happy together, so much so that the night before the wedding day she slept in the big bed on one side of me, with Dave on my other side. Paul Grabham spent the night at his father's house, which was just around the corner from us. He didn't have a stag do as he didn't have any friends; it turned out he was very unpopular.

February 16th dawned and Kirsty was up early and beside herself with excitement. After Sonya's husband John had driven her to the hairdressers to have her hair and make-up done, she came home and went upstairs to get ready, and I went to help. Suddenly she realised she didn't have anything borrowed, so I gave her a matching diamante necklace and earring set to wear.

Up in the bedroom she laughed and said that she had a surprise for Paul, that when the registrar asks 'Do you take this man to be your lawful wedded husband...' that she was going to say 'No.' I wished with all my heart that she hadn't been joking.

Finally, she was ready; she looked stunning in a long white satin gown with a sequined bandeau top and spaghetti straps; she was so tiny that her dress was actually a bridesmaid dress for an eleven-year-old. Her hair was swept up into a loose bundle with tendrils curling around her beautiful face, and a small diamond tiara nestled in her blond curls. The borrowed necklace hung around her slender neck, and a voile shawl kept the chill off on that cold February day.

As a surprise, Dave had booked a pink limousine to take us all to the local register office in Bridgend. It might not have been a princess carriage but it was close enough; Kirsty's face was a pure picture when it arrived – she really hadn't been expecting it and was over the moon. That pink limo looked huge on our little road but Kirsty was thrilled, clapping her hands together when she saw it, just like a little girl. Kirsty, Hayley, Sonya, four bridesmaids, Dave and I all got into the limo, and toasted Kirsty with the champagne that was chilled and waiting for us in the luxurious interior. Kirsty, beside herself with excitement, was hanging out of the window and waving at everyone she saw.

Even though Dave was Kirsty's stepfather, he was very proud to be giving her away, and he stood tall and handsome in his suit; Kirsty looked absolutely tiny walking beside him. The wedding went without a hitch, but all through it I had misgivings and wished it was Jonny that she was marrying. I videoed the whole thing, and when the time came for Kirsty to answer the question 'Do you take this man to be your lawful wedded husband...' I held my breath, hoping that she would say 'No'. But she didn't, she just gave me a secret smile and said 'I do.' I could've cried. Grabham now had Kirsty's name tattooed on his neck and he was wearing sparkly earrings.

After the ceremony, we went to the Green Acres pub and hotel for the reception; a sit-down dinner that Dave and I had paid for. His family were there, a scruffy bunch. At one point Sonya nudged me and whispered that it was like an episode of 'Shameless' and I must admit I had to agree. They had agreed to supply champagne for the toast and I was appalled when Grabham's father produced big dusty bottles of cheap plonk. Later in the afternoon Sonya and I went home to prepare a buffet for the evening as Paul Grabham had arranged a DJ for the night.

What a let-down it all was. When we got back to the pub, the DJ turned out to be Grabham's step-father, Stan; he didn't have the song that Kirsty had requested for her first dance, Alicia Keyes singing No One, so someone had to go and buy it. In fact, he had very little decent music at all. Afterwards, everyone came back to our house to continue with the buffet and the partying.

Kirsty and Grabham disappeared off to a hotel in Porthcawl for the night, and the next day they came to see us because Kirsty wanted to return the jewellery that she'd borrowed for the wedding. After they'd gone, Dave and I both agreed that Grabham had sneaky eyes, flicking here and there and missing nothing. We weren't happy about the wedding and we certainly didn't trust him.

Despite how we felt, the first few weeks of the marriage seemed peaceful and Kirsty appeared to be happy. She was really desperate to have a baby and every month she would ring me in tears when she realised that she hadn't conceived. After a few months, she began looking into fertility treatment, even though I told her to be patient, that these things take time.

We were still very close and Kirsty rang or texted, or sent me a Facebook message, every day. As the weeks went by I noticed that she wasn't her usual bright and chatty self when she rang; she sounded nervous, and I could hear Paul in the background telling her what to say. I wasn't happy about that – it just wasn't right. I remember thinking one time that he might actually be listening in on our phone calls because I asked Kirsty if he had a job yet and before she could speak I heard him in the background telling her to say that he had an interview lined up for a job as a postman.

On June 29th of that year, 2008, Sonya and John had a christening for their two daughters, Anais and Amelia Rose, in Coventry. We had agreed that Paul and Kirsty would get the coach from Swansea, and we would catch the same coach in Bridgend and travel the rest of the way together; it was close to Kirsty's birthday and I gave her a small silver bracelet with pink stones. Her eyes lit up when she saw it and she said she'd treasure it for ever and ever; I was so pleased that she loved it. When we arrived in Coventry, Dave and I had one suitcase between us, and Kirsty and Grabham had three; when I asked her why they had so many Kirsty laughed and said two of them were for her shoes. She really was a little shopaholic; she had more clothes and shoes than anybody else I knew.

Kirsty and Grabham stayed at my younger sister Kerry's house; Kirsty was really excited because she loved her Auntie Kerry, they were very close; Dave and I stayed at Sonya and John's house, to help with the food and the children the next day.

On the day of the christening, Dave looked after the children while Sonya, John, and I prepared the food and decorated the hall where the party was to be held afterwards. It was a wonderful day, I was in my element with all my family around me, and I loved the grandchildren to distraction. Kirsty videoed most of the christening service and later on the DJ played Valerie by Amy Winehouse, and Sonya, Hayley, Kirsty, and I danced to it. Little did we realise that it was the last time we would all dance together. Even now, when I hear that song, it brings a tear to my eye and a lump to my throat, remembering how happy we all were then.

After the christening party, Sonya and John took the opportunity for a little time alone and went to stay in a hotel for the night, while the rest of the family went back to their house. Dave and I were very happy to be babysitting for the night. We hadn't been back there for long when we heard shouting coming from the garden. We ran outside to see what was going on and there was a drunken Grabham, shouting at Kirsty and calling her a slag. It quickly escalated into the living room where my little granddaughters were huddled together in a corner, shaking and sobbing, absolutely terrified. Grabham was out of control, knocking furniture over and shouting. Dave was furious and got hold of Grabham, punching him in the head to stop his hysteria, and pushing him outside the front door. He told him not to dare talk to his daughter that way and that he was frightening his granddaughters, and locked him outside. Grabham was wild, banging on the door and kicking it, but we wouldn't let him back in. I was flabbergasted when Kirsty went out to him, especially after what he'd called her. They disappeared back to Kerry's house after that. I couldn't believe it.

When Sonya heard what had gone on, she told me that Kirsty had confided in her that a few weeks previously, when they were at a party; Paul had tried to strangle Kirsty. He pushed her onto a bed and sat on her stomach, put his hands around her throat and squeezed hard. He wouldn't let go, it was as if he was possessed, she'd been so terrified he was going to kill her that she lost control of her bladder and wet herself. Luckily someone came into the bedroom at that point and pulled Grabham off her. They'd only been married a few months at this stage but it seemed that all our fears were justified, Grabham was violent and untrustworthy and my heart ached for Kirsty.

I begged her to leave him, but she insisted that he was her husband and she had to take her vows seriously, to try to make it work. I remember saying to her, 'Kirsty, you've got to get away from him, you really, really have to. He sounds so dangerous, he's not right in the head. Babs, you've got to leave or he'll end up killing you and you'll be found in a ditch somewhere!' Dave and I were so furious with Grabham and his aggressive behaviour that we banned him from the house, telling him that we didn't like him and he wasn't welcome. But I worried about Kirsty's safety every single day. She was too kind-hearted and gentle and funny to protect herself against Grabham, who was basically a thug. Why couldn't she see that when the rest of us could see it so clearly?

Kirsty was such a lovely thoughtful girl, but she could be scatty too. Before she met Grabham, she lived in a rented flat and one evening she put candles around the bath to have a romantic evening with Jonny, her long-term boyfriend. The trouble was she forgot about the candles and they melted onto the plastic bath, damaging it so badly that she had to get it replaced before she could get her deposit back. Another time she put something under the grill and went to watch a television programme; she forgot all about it until someone stuck their head through the open window and asked if she knew her kitchen was on fire! And then there was the time she got the dog's chain stuck around her waist and we ended up having to call the fire brigade to cut it off. I could go on and on, there were so many incidents.

At a party one night Kirsty saw a tiny cat being abused; she loved animals and couldn't bear seeing it hurt, so she took it home, called it Princess, and it became her 'baby'. She was having trouble conceiving at the time, so it became a substitute baby for her. In hindsight, I'm so glad she didn't have a baby; I know that sounds harsh, but I would have had to bring the child up after she died and I don't know how I would have felt about that, knowing that a murderous thug like Grabham was its father. Then again, I'm sorry she didn't have a baby; I know I would have done my best by it and brought it up as a decent human being and it would have been like having a little bit of Kirsty still with us. My feelings on the subject are really mixed up.

Anyway, the cat suited her perfectly because both of them were tiny and that little cat adored her, following her around and letting her dress it up in little blingy costumes. She got it a pink hoody with 'Princess' in glittery letters on the back and little pink leather shoes and she used to walk it on a diamante lead. I thought it was hilarious. I remember one time when Dave and I went to visit her in the flat, we were just sitting around talking, chatting about nothing very exciting, when she suddenly looked at the cat and said, 'I'll need to get Princess some new shoes.' Well I just burst out laughing; it was as if she was speaking about a real child instead of a cat.

Kirsty loved older people and children, anyone vulnerable. I only found out after she died that she had a standing order to pay money to an African children's charity every month. My friend Mary lives in London with her husband Mark, but she was originally from Nairobi; they are staunch church-goers and do a lot of fundraising for charity. They've bought a plot of land in Nairobi and are hoping to build a shelter to help the whole community, including women in domestic violence situations and the homeless, and they're also going to make part of the shelter into a school to help the children. They also plan to have gardens where people can grow fruit and vegetables and it will help to feed people using the shelter. It will be a 'home for the helpless'. When they have raised enough money to realize their dream and to have their shelter built, they have asked if Dave and I will go over and present them with the cheque; I feel so honoured that they've asked us to do this because they are going to name it after Kirsty, and they plan to have photos of her on the walls. I think it's such a wonderful gesture, and it means that her memory will live on not only here but in another country as well. When we go to Nairobi to present the cheque Dave and I will stay for an extra week or so to help out, and I'm so looking forward to it.

Kirsty was such a gentle and affectionate girl who saw the good in everyone, and despite suffering at Paul's abusive hands, she loved him and felt that she could make him change his ways. She always forgave him and made excuses for him, saying he hadn't had a good upbringing or a decent role model so he didn't really know any better. She wanted to see the best in everyone, including him.

Even the discovery that he was cheating on her wasn't enough to make her leave him. It was some weeks after the strangling episode that she discovered Paul was seeing a woman he had met online. Kirsty was completely distraught, but once again she forgave him. Even when she found him on a 'dogging' website, arranging to meet other people, she still forgave him. I just couldn't understand how she could be so besotted with a man who would treat her so badly.

I hadn't heard of 'dogging' before this and had to find out what it was. I was really shocked to discover that it is about people having sex in public places while other people watch. So, Paul Grabham was arranging to meet strangers for sex while other strangers watched them. The whole idea made me shudder.

Kirsty was learning to drive and I was glad; I hoped it would give her some independence and a means of escape if she needed it. She passed her theory test very quickly, and was so excited and so confident of passing the actual driving test that she and Grabham went out and bought a little blue two-seater Suzuki. She said she was going to spray it pink as soon as she could. She really did love pink. She told me she'd borrowed money from a friend of the family to buy the car, and had promised to pay it back quickly and I knew she would, she'd always been reliable that way. Kirsty never did get to take her driving test and I don't know whether Grabham had a driving license or not, but he drove that car from the minute she got it and, as we later found out often used it to have sex with other women.

After a couple of months Dave and I realised that because we'd banned Grabham from our house we weren't seeing so much of Kirsty, so reluctantly we decided we'd let him into the house again and invited them over for the weekend. Seeing Kirsty was more important to us than keeping him out. When they came we went to a club in Porthcawl for a couple of drinks and a game of bingo, and there was a singer on afterwards. Grabham wouldn't leave Kirsty alone; he was all over her and it got really embarrassing; I even told them to go and get a room. Kirsty and I ended up dancing to a load of golden oldies and she was dead chuffed to be dancing to songs that she'd not heard before, and doing dances that she hadn't danced before, like the Jive and the Twist. We had such fun with me teaching her those fantastic dances.

About a month after that a letter for Grabham arrived at our house. Curious, we opened it and it turned out to be from a loan company. He'd used our address to take out a loan, and then stopped making the payments, but when we confronted him about it he denied everything. He was a bare-faced liar and Dave banned him from the house again.

In December Dave and I were gearing up for our Christmas holiday abroad, really looking forward to getting away from the cold weather and grey days. Alexandra Burke had just won X-Factor, and Joe Swash was crowned King of the Jungle in I'm a Celebrity Get Me Out of Here. Kirsty was looking forward to her first Christmas as a married woman and trying to decide on a present for Grabham. She came to see us off and waved goodbye excitedly, telling me everything was fine.

While Dave and I were away, Kirsty confided in Sonya that Paul was still using dogging websites on the internet and arranging to meet other women. She couldn't understand how he could cheat on her and lie to her constantly and she'd had enough. She was determined to get away and make a fresh start and she said she was going to move to Coventry as soon as she could. When we got back and Sonya told me this in confidence I was so pleased; at last my pink princess was coming to her senses.

After that Christmas holiday, Kirsty came to see us; she told us that Dave and I had been right about Grabham and she admitted that she couldn't cope with his behaviour any longer and was going to leave him. I can't tell you how delighted and relieved I was. The sooner she left him the better it would be for all concerned. I encouraged her to get out of the marriage as quickly as she could, hugging her and telling her she was doing the right thing. We told her we would help her in any way we could. We all ended up in tears; Kirsty because she was so unhappy that her marriage was over, and us with relief that her marriage was over.

I was counting the days until she left him, so it was a huge shock when she said she was going to give him another chance. We asked her why and pleaded with her, telling her she was crazy to go back to him after what he'd done, that he would never change, but again, she wouldn't listen. It was so frustrating.

Another couple of months passed and, although nothing had changed for the better, Kirsty was still with Grabham and we were still terribly worried.

Then something strange happened. On Saturday March 14, 2009, I woke up and found a huge, purple bruise covering the whole of my stomach. I wasn't in pain and I hadn't had any kind of medical problem or injury. But it looked alarming. It was so strange that I mentioned it to Sonya when we spoke, and I took a picture of it and sent it to her. Sonya was alarmed and insisted I go to the doctor. I did, on the Monday, and he was flummoxed and said he hadn't seen anything like it before. He had no explanation for what it was. Later, looking back, I wondered if it had been a sign of what was to come; my body telling me that the baby I had carried under that bruised area was in trouble.

Eight days after the bruise appeared, on Mother's Day, March 22, Kirsty came to visit. Paul dropped her off then went for a drive until the visit was over. She didn't look herself that day. She had no make-up on, which was really unusual for her, she was wearing jogging bottoms and a hooded top, and her hair was tied back. She usually looked immaculate in pretty clothes, but that day it seemed as if she didn't care how she looked and she wasn't her usual bubbly chatty self, she seemed subdued and downbeat. We chatted a little about Coronation Street and Big Brother, because we both watched them, and then we heard on the news that Jade Goody had just passed away and we talked about how tragic it was that she died so young and how terrible it was for her two little boys.

I kept thinking that the sparkle had gone out of my lovely pink princess and she looked so sad and lost. As far as I was concerned, the time for her to leave Grabham couldn't come around quick enough. Why was she still hesitating? She seemed nervous, and kept looking out of the window to see if he had come back and was waiting for her.

She gave me a huge box of chocolates and a card, and then she crouched down beside Dave and said 'This is for you, Dad. I know it's not Father's Day yet but you can have it now.' It was a bottle of unusual alcohol that she had bought at a fete.

The next thing I knew, Grabham had pulled up outside and beeped the horn. Kirsty jumped up saying, 'I have to go now, I don't want to keep Paul waiting' and headed for the back door. I went with her as far as the driveway and gave her a big hug and a kiss, cuddling her as tight as I could. If I had known that this would be the last time I would ever see her alive I would never have let her go.

After I waved her off I went back into the house; Dave said we should try and get Kirsty to come and stay with us for a break since she looked so tired and unhappy and I totally agreed.

CHAPTER FOUR
THE DISAPPEARANCE

As the week went by Kirsty continued phoning and sending me texts and messages on Facebook. She told me she was staying at a friend's brother's house as she was again thinking of leaving Grabham and maybe going to live in Coventry; she liked it there and would at least be near her sisters. I kept my fingers crossed that she would actually leave him this time and move away, because I could see how unhappy he was making her. We offered to go to her flat and collect her things, and then go to Sonya's in Coventry with her, but she said no, she needed to arrange a few things first.

She had recently started going to bingo and was having a lucky streak because she kept winning – nothing life changing, but enough to buy a few new clothes and some make-up. I told her that I was going to Castle Bingo in Bridgend on Friday to see if I could win anything; I had never been there before so I thought I'd give it a go. When the Friday came, I messaged Kirsty on Facebook to have a good night out as she'd told me she was going out with friends, and had been out shopping to buy new clothes. I told her I was going to the bingo. She replied, saying 'Do you want some of my luck?' Those were the last words I ever heard from her.

I found out afterwards that she had phoned and asked Grabham to collect her from her friend's house because she wanted to get dressed at home and put her nail varnish on. He picked her up and took her to the flat and, somehow, he ended up going out with her as well. They went to La Tosca's where Kirsty had a sangria and he had a vodka, then they both went to a nightclub called Play to meet Kirsty's friends. Later in the evening Grabham, out of his face on drink and cocaine, knocked over a table in the club spilling everyone's drinks. He and Kirsty had words, she told him to go home and he did. He got a taxi and neighbours saw him get out of it, so drunk and drugged up that he couldn't even walk properly. He managed to stagger into the house and up the stairs to their flat then, as we later found out, he rang his drug dealer to bring more cocaine to the flat and he started drinking more vodka.

Kirsty stayed on at the club with her friends, then they all moved on to one of their houses; after a while Kirsty and Paloma went to Paloma's house, and whilst they were there Kirsty told her that she was going to leave Grabham but had to plan it properly and leave him at the right time. When Kirsty said she was going to get a taxi home Paloma tried to persuade her to stay there with her, but Kirsty was adamant that she wanted to go home. When the taxi arrived Paloma told Kirsty to make sure she sent a text to let her know that she'd got home alright.

Kirsty was chatting away to the taxi driver on the way home, telling him how fed up she was with men and that they were all a waste of time. When they pulled up outside the flat she remarked that the light was off, 'Good, it looks like he's not in so I'll have the bed to myself.' Neighbours heard Kirsty going up the concrete steps that she had to climb to get to the flat, calling to her little cat, 'Princess, mummy is home my little darling'. Once inside she texted Paloma, as she had promised, and said 'Paul is in the living room laying on the sofa, but I got home safe.' That was the last time anyone heard from her.

I wasn't too worried when Kirsty didn't phone or text me the next day. Knowing that she'd been out the night before with her friends and that it was more than likely that they didn't get home until the early hours, I knew she was probably having a lie-in. I did phone her but there was no answer, so I sent a text message asking if she was okay and if she had enjoyed her night out, and settled down to watch Primeval, a series I loved. I didn't hear from her all day, but I wasn't too worried. But when I tried phoning her again on Sunday afternoon and there was still no answer, and she hadn't answered my text, I began to feel anxious. Kirsty always answered texts sooner rather than later, and I hadn't heard from her in two days which was almost unheard of. The television was on, but I wasn't really watching; all I could think about was Kirsty.

She had friends everywhere and I started wondering whether she had gone to see one of them for a few days so she could have time to think, time to get her head straight and decide what to do. I was so worried that I started asking all her friends on Facebook if they knew where she was or if anyone had seen her since the Friday night; I said if they had seen or heard from her or knew where she'd gone, could they send me a private message, just so that I would know she was okay. Then the lad that Kirsty had stayed with the week before, her friends' brother, rang and told me about the argument that Kirsty and Grabham had on the Friday night in the nightclub. He said that Grabham had been so out of order, that Kirsty asked him to leave and go home.

I couldn't sleep that night because of the worry. I got out of bed about five o'clock on the Monday morning, desperate to phone Kirsty and wishing the time away so that I could ring her. I was really worried; I kept thinking that if I didn't hear from her it would be three days since she'd contacted me. At half past eight the phone rang, and I thought, 'Thank God, that must be Kirsty'. It was Grabham, asking if I'd seen her.

'What do you mean, "have I seen her?"' I asked him.

'She was with you. You both went to a night club and for a drink together on Friday night. Did you argue?'

'No. We were fine. We had a good night and there were no arguments. Why would you even think that? Can you just try and get in touch with her and let me know where she is?'

Why was he lying? I really didn't trust him.

'Where do you think she is?' I asked. 'And where has she been between Friday night and now?'

'I don't know, she might be at a friend's house watching the rugby. There was a big match on at the weekend. All I know is she took some money from the computer desk, about £160, but she didn't take her debit card, so she can't be too far away.'

I thought that was a bit odd; why would she do that when she was due to get some money paid into her account the next day, Tuesday?

'And,' he continued. 'She took her pink hair straighteners.'

'Did she take a hair brush?'

'Um … no, it's still here.'

'That's strange. Did she take anything else?'

'Well, she'd ironed some clothes and left them on the bottom of the bed. They're gone too.'

This didn't make sense to me, it didn't feel right at all. Why on earth would Kirsty take money but leave her debit card? And why would she take her straighteners but not her hairbrush? She always had a hair bobble on her wrist and would have taken her hairbrush and just put her long hair into a pony tail. And as for the clothes being ironed and left on the bottom of the bed, that didn't sit right with me at all because Kirsty only ironed her clothes as and when she needed them. I'd never known her to iron anything in advance. And I mean – never!

I told Grabham to contact the police right away and report Kirsty missing. I really didn't trust him, and didn't think he would ring them. In actual fact, he did, but just to be on the safe side I rang them myself and explained that Kirsty had gone missing, nobody had seen her since Friday night, and that her husband had at one time tried to strangle her. I didn't hold back, I said that he was violent, a compulsive liar, and he was definitely not to be trusted. I told them about the friend's brother phoning and telling me about the night out and the argument, and Grabham then denying it, and about the things that he said were missing from the flat.

While Dave and I sat there waiting to hear back from the police, not knowing what to do with ourselves, two police officers went to visit Grabham at Kirsty's flat and ask him a few questions. They told me later that he did his best to explain what happened and that he had been extremely helpful.

I also rang Sonya and Hayley to let them know what was happening. Sonya rang Grabham herself and got the same story about the debit card and the hair straighteners. We were all suspicious of him. I texted Kirsty repeatedly after that, and left voicemail messages asking her to text me back or ring me, but there was no reply.

I was sick with worry; maybe it was a mother's instinct, or some sort of bond because we had always been so close, but I just knew something had happened to her, although I never, ever thought for one minute that my precious daughter was dead.

By Tuesday I was frantic; where the heck was she? Kirsty would definitely have got in touch with me if she was able to, because she knew how much I worried. I remember one time when I hadn't heard from her for three days, I ended up phoning the police and asking them to go to her flat to see if she was okay. Luckily, she was, she had run out of credit on her mobile phone and didn't have a landline at the time. I told her that if that ever happened again, she had to go to a phone box and reverse the charges just to let me know she was okay. It never did happen again, that was the only time she had been out of touch for more than a day. Until now.

We didn't dare leave the house, in case she phoned. We sat, drinking endless cups of tea, waiting and watching the hours tick slowly by. I couldn't sleep or eat, I felt so desperate to know that she was alright. On the Wednesday afternoon, the police called in to see us, to tell us that Kirsty's debit card had been used in Bridgend at lunchtime. I felt a surge of happiness. Surely it meant she was alright? I convinced myself that if Kirsty was in Bridgend using her debit card then she was okay. For a few brief hours I had real hope that she would soon come home.

I found out later that Grabham had used the card to get cash and spent all of Kirsty's money on drink and drugs and having parties in the flat.

After the police had gone Grabham rang to tell me that Kirsty must have been back to the flat while he was out, as he had just noticed that her toothbrush had gone.

'Didn't you notice this before now?'

'No, I didn't. I just said, didn't I? I only just noticed.'

'So basically, you haven't brushed your teeth since Friday?'

'Of course I have! Our toothbrushes are on different shelves – I've got special toothpaste from the dentist so we make sure they don't get mixed up.'

This didn't ring true to me. Every couple that I know keep their toothbrushes together. Despite all my worries, I had been convinced that Kirsty would turn up with an explanation for her disappearance. But at that moment my blood chilled. For the first time I had serious doubts about what might have happened to my pink princess.

Desperate and needing to do something, anything, on the Wednesday after Kirsty disappeared I put a large advert in the local newspaper, begging for anyone who had any information about Kirsty, or who had seen her, to let the police know that she was safe and well. It was an emotional appeal, explaining how concerned I was and how out of character it was for Kirsty to disappear. I thought maybe if Kirsty saw it she would realise how worried we were and text or ring us to put us out of our misery, but the phones remained quiet.

Sonya and Hayley were phoning constantly to see if there was any news. I was always happy to hear from them and we talked about it over and over, wondering where she could be.

By Thursday we still hadn't heard anything. Then in the early evening, I glanced out of the window and saw a police car slow down outside. Detective Neil Jones, in charge of the case, got out of the car with another officer and came towards the front door. The look on his face was deadly serious, as if he was on a mission. Suddenly my heart started hammering and my legs felt shaky.

The bell rang and I heard Dave go to open the front door, heard voices in the hallway, and then they were coming into the room.

'Mrs Broomfield...'

'Have you found her?'

'No. No, we haven't found her, but why don't you take a seat?'

'No, just tell me. Please. What is it...?'

'We wanted you to know that we've arrested Paul Grabham on suspicion of murder...'

I felt as if I'd been punched in the stomach, I was sick and shaky; my legs went weak and I just plopped down onto the couch. Dave was immediately beside me, an arm around my shoulder.

This was the first time that anyone had suggested that Kirsty might be dead. He was still talking and I struggled to take in what he was saying. '...we have to ask you not to talk about the arrest because it could well jeopardize a court case. I really must impress on you that you have to keep this information to yourselves. If the press get hold of it...'

'I don't understand,' I said, confused. 'How can you arrest him for murder if you haven't found her? She's still out there somewhere...' Thoughts raced through my mind. I couldn't bear to think of anything bad happening to my beautiful daughter, but where was she? I felt as though I was dreaming. In my wildest imaginings, I hadn't expected this. I had told myself that Kirsty had gone away to lie low and escape Paul. Now, despite the fact that no body had been found, that flicker of hope was fading.

After Neil Jones left, Dave and I sat together on the couch, holding hands, as we listened to the other officer who had arrived at the same time. He introduced himself as John Quinn, the Police Family Liaison Officer and he explained that he would be our contact with the police, he would keep us up to date every step of the way and he also had questions to ask us. They needed to build a complete picture of Kirsty, to try to fill in the time leading up to her disappearance. He said that we could ask him questions or ring him at any time, he would be there to give us support and help in any way he could. He gave us his mobile number, and the number of another officer who would also be our PFLO. John Quinn said he would deal with the press and we mustn't talk to the media at all, it must all go through him. Any remark we made that the media got a hold of could affect a future court case, so we really needed to be aware of what we said and who we spoke to.

He told us that during the course of their investigations, they had discovered Kirsty had tried to make a 999 call in the early hours of Saturday morning, but the call had been stopped before it could be connected. This was suspicious in itself, and one of the reasons they'd arrested Paul Grabham. He emphasized again that this information was for us alone and to be kept out of the press.

While we thought about all this he made us a cup of tea, then putting one on the coffee table in front of Dave, he asked me to go into the dining room with him because he wanted to talk to me privately. I couldn't think why because Dave and I have no secrets, but I went with him anyway and sat at the table waiting, wondering what he wanted. He put the cup of tea down in front of me and sat opposite.

'I've got some news, but I wanted to tell you alone first.' He took a sip of his tea before continuing. 'Did you know that Kirsty was a prostitute?' He gazed at me steadily.

'What? A what...? No, no she wasn't! Why would you say something like that?'

'She worked at the massage parlour, didn't she? Mystiques in Bridgend.'

'No! What are you talking about? She's a glamour model. Why would you think she did anything else?' My heart was racing; how could he talk about my Kirsty like that?

He nodded. 'I was pretty sure you didn't know, but it's true. Paul Grabham was a prostitute at Mystiques. That's where they met.'

'No, no. You've made a mistake. They met at a party. You've got it all wrong. My Kirsty would never do something like that. Never!' I jumped up and rushed into the other room, to Dave. 'You'll never believe what he's telling me. He's saying that Kirsty was a...was a...prostitute!' I spat the word out. 'What a load of nonsense, it's rubbish. I don't know where he gets off talking about her like that.' I was distraught, completely shocked, and I started crying. Talk about a bolt from the blue!

'Come on Cathy, sit down here with me. We'll get to the bottom of this.' Dave was urging me onto the couch next to him while John Quinn stood in the doorway waiting for me to calm down. 'Come on love, let's hear what the man has to say.'

I sat next to Dave, holding his hand, struggling to get my breathing under control. I was trembling and felt sick inside, trying to get my head around what I was being told. John Quinn sat back on the armchair opposite us and started talking again about the investigation, telling us what they'd discovered. He was talking about Kirsty, talking about Grabham, talking about the sex trade that they were involved in. What sex trade? I simply couldn't believe what I was hearing. He said that Kirsty may have been a part-time glamour model, but she was also one of the working girls at the massage parlour.

His words kept going around in my brain. Kirsty a prostitute? My Kirsty? A prostitute? I was horrified, I couldn't speak, just sat and listened with disbelief. So many thoughts were running around my head, but the main theme was 'This isn't my Kirsty, she would never have willingly sold her body for sex. Never! What is this man talking about?' Kirsty wasn't a prostitute.

There are no words to describe the shock and confusion I felt listening to what he said about my beautiful Kirsty. Sadly, in the months to come, I had to accept that everything he said was true. My pink princess was indeed a glamour model, and I had some lovely photos of her to show that, but she also led another life, a secret life that I knew nothing about.

John Quinn asked me if I'd go on television to make an appeal to the public for anyone with any information to come forward, anyone who'd seen Kirsty since Saturday morning. He said there would be an actress playing Kirsty and they would film a reconstruction of her last movements hoping it might jog somebody's memory. But I knew I wouldn't be able to do it, I was a nervous wreck, sick with worry, how could they expect me to sit in front of television cameras and do that without breaking down? Maybe Sonya could do it?

We rang Sonya and asked if she would come to South Wales and do the television appeal; she sounded tearful but she agreed. She would be with us as soon as she could, she said, probably on Monday because she needed to sort out childcare. I was so grateful and relieved. My brave girl. My brave, supportive Sonya.

John Quinn left soon after that, with another warning not to talk to the press. He said he'd be back first thing in the morning. He would let us know the arrangements for the television appeal and they would set it up as soon as possible.

The next morning, Friday, Dave went out to get some milk and the newspaper. When he got back he had at least a dozen newspapers with him, and without a word he started spreading them out on the table. It took me a minute to realise what I was reading. 'Cops Fear Missing Kirsty Murdered' was one of the headlines and the others were all similar. It was horrible. I sank down onto a chair and started crying. This seemed to make it all so real, but I was still in denial, thinking Kirsty couldn't be dead, there was no way. Who would hurt my little girl, let alone murder her? She was so gentle, and so loved.

The newspapers said that someone had been arrested in connection with the murder of model Kirsty Grabham but it didn't name anyone. We knew, obviously, but – oh my God, MURDER! It was really beginning to sink in and I became slightly hysterical. The doctor was called out and he gave me some anxiety pills, saying they would take the edge off the pain, but they made no difference at all to the awful feeling of foreboding that I had, as if the ground was falling away from under my feet. I ended up throwing them in the dustbin; I wanted to be fully aware of all that was going on around me, not drugged up.

Over the next two days we suffered a whole weekend of lurid headlines in the local and national press, and we even had journalists ringing to ask us who it was that had been arrested. I don't even know how they got our phone number because we are ex-directory, but of course we refused to say anything. At the same time there were constant phone calls to Hayley and Sonya, keeping them up to date, each of us trying to keep the other calm. But the worst was yet to come.

CHAPTER FIVE
THE FINDING

On the morning of Monday April 6, nine days after Kirsty's disappearance, Dave and I were sitting, stony-faced, drinking coffee, and staring at nothing as if we were zombies. We were barely sleeping, barely functioning, just waiting for news. I still hoped beyond hope that Kirsty was lying low somewhere, but if she was, then surely she would have seen her face splashed all over the front pages of the newspapers. Deep down I knew that she would have been in touch if she was able, a phone call, a text, anything.

Sonia rang to say she was setting off from Coventry, with her husband John and Hayley. I was looking forward to seeing her and Hayley and giving them a hug. It would be comforting to have my other girls with me, I knew this was a terrible ordeal for them too.

A couple of hours later I heard a car slow down outside and then car doors slamming. I got up and looked out of the window; there was Detective Neil Jones, and our FPLO John Quinn, standing next to an unmarked police car, talking quietly. My heart started thumping and I felt a bit sick. Why were they here? I wasn't expecting them till later in the day when Sonya had arrived. They were going to come and discuss the television appeal.

They turned and started walking towards the house. I could see the grim look on their faces and the droop of their shoulders, and I suddenly realised they had more bad news. I didn't want to know, I didn't want to hear it; the blood rushed through my ears and I covered them, closed my eyes, and shook my head trying to block it all out. Oh god, oh god, oh god... The next thing Dave was rubbing my arm and leading me to the couch. I opened my eyes, and there were tears running down my face as I looked at the two policemen who were standing in our living room, looking huge and blocking out the light. I was trembling as Dave tried to gently push me down onto the couch; but I wanted to be standing for this, whatever it was they had to tell us. I took a deep breath and braced myself, but I still wasn't prepared for what they said next.

'The body of a young woman has been found, in some undergrowth. We believe it could be Kirsty...'

I think I might have screamed, and collapsed onto the couch. 'No no no no...' Then, in total shock, before they had even finished speaking, I started phoning everyone I could think of, my sisters, my friends, screaming down the phone that Kirsty was dead. Dead! She's dead! And then I fell into a heap, sobbing uncontrollably.

At that same time, John, Sonya and Hayley were still on their way down from the Midlands. Driving along the M4, about two miles from where we lived in Bridgend, they saw an area beside the motorway that had been cordoned off; there were a lot of police cars and police vans and reporters and photographers everywhere. Another woman had gone missing at about that time and Sonya did actually say to John that maybe they'd found her, never dreaming that the person they'd found was actually her little sister. Hayley was on the back seat, drinking from a bottle of wine; she was really worried about Kirsty and didn't know how to cope, didn't know what to do with herself.

When they got to the house, they found me slumped on the floor in a corner, arms wrapped around myself, howling in pain and sobbing for Kirsty.

We were all distraught. We spent the night weeping and talking and going over and over it. Maybe they had it wrong, maybe it wasn't Kirsty; could it be the other woman who had gone missing? But if that was the case, where was Kirsty?

Hayley got progressively drunker as the night wore on, and the more she drank the more she wept. It was unbearable to see, but I was trying to cope with my own pain and didn't know how to comfort her. She didn't want to go to the mortuary with us the next day, and we decided it would be better if John took her back to the Midlands, away from the whole scene.

Dave, Sonya and I were picked up in the morning and taken to the mortuary. I dreaded going in to see her, and yet I had to be sure. Was this going to be my baby? Could I bear it if it was? I shook from head to toe as we stepped into the room where the body lay.

I forced myself to look. This wasn't my Kirsty. No, definitely not. I didn't recognise her at all. The face that confronted us was badly battered; the eyes were so bruised and swollen I couldn't even see the eyelashes, and the jaw was broken. There were fingerprints on her cheeks from where she'd been grabbed, and her nose was grazed and broken. Her face was covered in scratches and there was blood matted in her hair.

This girl was so badly beaten that she was beyond recognition. But Dave and Sonya said it was Kirsty. I didn't believe them, but then Dave very gently told me to look at the eyebrows, and I did eventually agree that they were very similar to Kirsty's – the only part of her that looked like it might have been Kirsty. I just couldn't believe that this was my daughter though, my Kirsty, my beautiful pink princess. We weren't allowed to touch the body in case we contaminated any evidence, so I asked to look at her wrist, looking for the small star tattoo, the same one that Hayley had: 'sistars'. That would have been the proof for me, but the technician refused to lift her arm.

I so wanted to hold her, to kiss her cheek, maybe then I would believe it was her, but the sight of that bruised and battered face terrified poor Sonya, so we left the room. Suddenly I knew I needed to see my Kirsty one last time and I went back in on my own and said a private and final goodbye to her. Even then I didn't want to believe it was really her, but everyone said it was, so I had to take their word for it.

That day, April 7th, would have been my mum's birthday if she had still been alive, but she died very young, aged just 67. When I got outside I looked up to the sky and said 'Well mum, it's your birthday today and you are getting the best present ever sent up to you.' I knew that she would look after my beautiful Kirsty – if that was, indeed, who was lying on that cold mortuary slab.

It was only after we'd been to identify her body that we discovered that she had been found in a suitcase beside the M4, just a couple of miles from where we lived. A lorry driver who had stopped for a break saw the bulging black suitcase in the brush and climbed down the embankment to investigate. He opened it and the first thing he saw was a hand. At first, he thought it was a mannequin, but then he saw the ring on the finger and rang the police.

I couldn't stop thinking about what Kirsty went through that night. Was she shouting for me? I was sure she would want her mum. Was she still alive when he stuffed her in that tiny suitcase? Did she know what was happening? I was heartbroken and my mind wouldn't stop whirring, thinking over and over about everything that had happened to her.

Grabham had driven all the way from Swansea to Bridgend with my poor Kirsty in the car, and dumped her so close to home, on an embankment at the side of the M4 amongst all the trees and bushes. He obviously thought she wouldn't be found for months. We were lucky that the lorry driver had chosen that particular spot to stop his lorry for a break, otherwise we might never have found her.

The next day, April 8, Paul Grabham appeared at Swansea Magistrates Court. None of the family could bring ourselves to go; we couldn't bear to see the murdering psychopath who had put our poor Kirsty through such a terrible frenzied attack. In fact, Hayley couldn't deal with any of it and had started drinking to blot it out, weeping and moaning, 'Where's my Stig? I want Stig.'

Reporters from the papers, radio and television were there and they said he was very quiet and didn't look at anyone as the cameras flashed in his face. He was screamed at and threatened by some of Kirsty's friends and members of the public; they were raging at what he had done. He just kept a steely look on his face the whole time and it wasn't until they were inside the court that the press realised it was Kirsty's husband who was being charged. Setting the scene for what was going to be a huge investigation and trial, Grabham was charged with Kirsty's murder. He didn't speak except to confirm his name, and he was remanded in custody until April 17.

In the days that followed, armfuls of flowers and cards were left at the spot where Kirsty had been found and we planted a pink rosebush there for her. I knew that she had gone, but my heart refused to accept it. Every time the phone rang or there was a knock on the door I jumped up to answer, hoping against hope that it would be her.

About a week after we'd been to the mortuary to identify Kirsty's body, the coroner came to the house to talk to us. Dave ushered him into the front room and I made him a cup of tea, then we all sat down. I wasn't really sure what he wanted to talk to us about, so when he started talking about organ donation I felt a bit stunned.

'Have you had time to think about what you would like to do with your daughter's organs?' He looked at me, quietly waiting for an answer, and Dave gently took my hand and held it firmly in his.

'No, I haven't... didn't really think...'

'We haven't replaced the brain yet, from the post mortem, so...'

'What?' I jumped up, shocked to the core, and screamed at him. 'Put it back! Put my baby's brain back! How dare you? How dare you do that to her? Put it back! Please, just put it back!' I sank down onto the couch again, sobbing, and Dave put an arm around me. I felt sick thinking of my child lying on a mortuary slab with bits of her body missing.

'I'm so sorry, I thought you would have realized.'

'Well we didn't, we didn't realize, nobody told us that, that...'

'It's standard procedure, I'm sorry. Somebody should have talked to you, given you information, leaflets to read through.'

'Nobody mentioned it to us.' Dave stroked my back soothingly, trying to calm me down, while he spoke to the coroner. 'It's a bit of a shock you see, just give us a moment to get used to the idea. We're just ordinary people, we don't know how these things work, so just give us a couple of minutes.'

'Of course.'

The coroner sat quietly and drank his tea, looking through some paperwork he had taken from a briefcase, while Dave soothed me and I gradually calmed down. It was bad enough, imagining all the things that Grabham had done to my beautiful girl, but now there were more horrific images crowding my mind.

As I calmed myself and though about Kirsty and how thoughtful and caring she was, I knew that if she could she would want to help others, especially babies, even after her death. After several minutes I took a deep breath and faced the coroner. 'Okay, let's start again. You were asking if we'd thought about organ donation?'

'That's correct.'

'I know my daughter would be happy to donate whatever she can. So...what would you take?'

'Usually we would take things like the brain, eyes, heart, trachea, uterus, bowel – there is so much that we can use to help others, it's impossible to list. But most organs have to be harvested within hours of death for them to be viable for transplant. This case is slightly different in that the time for the organs to be viable have long gone. But, we can still use various organs for research and this is just as important and valuable as transplanting them into other patients.'

'Okay.' I took a deep breath and looked at Dave for a moment. My mind was whirling, confused thoughts were spinning in and out of my head;

- This is what Kirsty would want isn't it?
- Sure, and it's the right thing to do.
- If we do it, my baby would be missing bits of her body!

- She would be helping others though.
- But I don't want her to be buried with parts missing.
- Yes, but think of the number of people she could help. Maybe even babies. She'd like that.
- But she's <u>my</u> baby and I want her back. I don't want her to be…

'Well, what do you think Mrs Broomfield?' The coroner interrupted my thoughts. I felt pressured to make an immediate decision, and my mind still spun as he continued. 'There are a couple of ways it can be done; would you like me to explain them to you?' He talked through the choices and the more I heard the more I became certain which option Kirsty would take, so I made the decision to donate her organs for scientific purposes; that way she would be helping others, and we could have the funeral straight away.

After I signed the paperwork for organ donation and the coroner had gone, I sat and wept. I wish I'd had more time to think about the decision, to talk it over properly with Dave and Hayley and Sonya. It was such a big decision I felt the whole family should have been able to talk about it, instead of having to make an instant decision.

Why had the coroner come out of the blue to ask us about this, and to tell us almost immediately that they hadn't replaced Kirsty's brain? It was so shocking to think of. Someone should have mentioned organ donation, talked us through it and given us leaflets or some kind of information to take home, so that we could consider our options. If I hadn't known Kirsty was such a generous person and would want to help others, it would have been an impossible decision at such an overwhelming time.

Now, whenever Dave and I pass by Heath Hospital in Cardiff, which is where Kirsty had been in the mortuary, I always say 'My little Kirsty is still in there – well, at least some parts of her are,' and I bless her.

Kirsty and Paul's flat had been examined and blood spatters were found throughout. Grabham had strangled and battered her, then caved in the back of her head. He attempted to cut her in half, which didn't work, and then he forced her into a small suitcase. He put the case in the boot of Kirsty's car, then drove down the M4 and threw the suitcase into some bushes beside the motorway. He then went back to the flat to clean up. It had been such a violent attack there were even blood spatters on the ceiling; he had painted over these before getting on the internet and looking at dogging sites again, and later in the day he went off in search of sex, and then had some friends over to the flat for a party.

Kirsty had kept a journal; the police had found it when they searched the flat, and they showed me a funeral plan that she had written. It was a list of ten things she wanted to happen at her funeral. Some of the things she asked for were a pink coffin and pink flowers, for everyone to wear pink, and drink pink champagne. And she didn't want to be buried with her engagement and wedding rings.

I was absolutely stunned; had she known she was going to die? She must have been so scared to have even thought along those lines but she must have had some sort of understanding that the situation she was in could lead to her death, she must have known what he was eventually going to do to her.

I found out later that when the CID who interviewed Grabham told him that Kirsty's body had been found and that she was no longer alive, he just shrugged his shoulders as if to say 'so what?'. The officers said that if the shoe was on the other foot and they were in Grabham's position and it was their wife that had been found, they would have gone mad and thrown chairs and tables, screamed and cried. They just couldn't get over his reaction; he displayed no pity, not a flicker of remorse, nothing at all. And all Grabham would say when he was arrested was 'What?', 'Where?', 'Why?', and 'No comment' every time he was asked a question, and this continued right up until the case went to trial.

I also discovered that the police found Kirsty's mobile phone in Grabham's pocket; so the whole time after she disappeared, and I thought she was still alive somewhere, when I was frantically texting and ringing and leaving messages for her to get in touch, Paul Grabham – knowing she was already dead – was reading the texts and listening to the voicemails and carrying on with the pretence that she was still alive but had left him.

Our other FPLO was a lovely officer called Emma Hughes. She went to Kirsty's flat just before the funeral and got a pink dress for Kirsty to wear in her coffin; I was so pleased, because until then nobody had been allowed into the flat as forensics were still in there investigating.

Kirsty's funeral was on April 27 and we followed her plan as best we could. The church was so packed that people spilled onto the pavement outside; the police had cordoned off the road and reporters, photographers and television cameras lined the barriers. Outside the church there were mountains of flowers. Six of Kirsty's girlfriends, dressed in black trousers and pink tops, carried her coffin, and at the end of the service Hayley, sobbing, released two white doves.

Emma was very good with us and we were so grateful for all her help. When the trial started she collected us every single day and drove us from Bridgend to Swansea Crown Court, and back again; that poor woman must have been worn out.

I was dreading seeing Paul Grabham, but it was mid-July before I first set eyes on him, the monster who had so callously murdered my beloved daughter. I was sitting in the courtroom waiting for him to be brought up by the Reliance officers to stand in the dock. I had wondered what my reaction would be when I saw him; I was sweating and shaking almost uncontrollably, and my stomach felt like it had been put through a mangle, just like my heart.

When he came into the courtroom I actually thought I was going to vomit; he saw me right away and started staring at me, and I stared right back at him. He wouldn't stop staring at me with those dark wicked eyes that had watched my daughter die, I felt he was looking into my soul; but I wasn't going to let him intimidate me and I continued to stare right back at him. In the end he looked away first. I'd got the better of him. I know to some people that might sound childish but the victory I felt at that moment gave me a teeny-weeny bit of satisfaction.

I was overwhelmed by the hatred I felt towards this excuse for a human being. I wanted to rip him apart, grab his face and gouge his eyes out. He was the one responsible for all the heartache that my family and I had had to endure, and he had robbed us of a precious member of our family.

One of Kirsty's friends, Julie Thomas, sat next to me in court that day, holding my hand tightly. I had got to know Julie pretty well and really liked and respected her; she had been one of the pall bearers at Kirsty's funeral. She told me that she would be with me every step of the way during the court trial, and I was so glad she was there; she really was a kind and genuine person and I knew I could trust her.

At this point Grabham was wearing glasses; I'd never seen him wearing glasses before. What was that all about?

Did he think that wearing spectacles would make him look innocent? All he did that day was answer to confirm his name and address. Greg Taylor QC said he had been informed by Grabham's barrister, Geraint Walters, that the defence case was a complete denial of participation in any way. According to the defence, the court heard that Grabham did not commit this murder and he was not present in the flat, he was not responsible for anything that went on in that flat or subsequently in the place where the body was found.

"What a bloody liar!" I was thinking through all of this. The murdering bastard had been seen by the neighbours getting out of a taxi, rotten drunk, and going in the stairwell that led up to the flat. How in God's name could he deny this?

The court heard that this was the biggest investigation being undertaken by South Wales police, and there was a lot of forensic and scientific work to be done. Two police offers were working full time to analyse CCTV images gathered during the investigation, and they still had more people to interview; in all, over 600 people were interviewed. It was going to take a good few months to gather all the evidence and interview everyone. So it was decided that Grabham would appear in court again in November. This seemed a long way off, why couldn't they deal with it all quicker? But the police reminded us several times over the next months that this was one of the biggest cases that had ever been handled by South Wales police, and we had to be patient.

I just wanted it to be over, and in the state of mind I was in, I wanted it done straight away. Grabham was guilty and needed to be punished as soon as possible, he needed to be locked up for a long, long time because no woman was safe as long as he roamed the streets. I was just glad he was locked up in the meantime. I couldn't believe it when the judge said to Grabham that he was sorry for the inconvenience the delay might cause him. What was that all about? The judge was apologising to the man who had murdered my little girl; he deserved to be in prison. I know, innocent until proven guilty – but the evidence against Grabham was overwhelming.

I dreamed of torturing Grabham to make him feel a little bit of what my daughter must have gone through when he battered and strangled her to death. How dare he? Who gave him the right to hurt my Kirsty the way he had? It was, and still is, so hard to imagine what my sweet dear daughter went through that night; my god, she must have been terrified. Did she cry out for me? Did she know that she was going to die at the hands of her so-called loving husband? The poor girl never stood a chance against that evil bastard; he must have battered her the way he would a punch bag, and pulled her about like a rag doll. I kept thinking of the state of Kirsty's face and how it was in that cold, clinical, mortuary. All the damage he had done to it, the pain and fear she had obviously gone through before she died. It was beyond words.

Why hadn't I been able to protect her? Why, oh why, didn't I tell her to come and live with me for a week or so until she had got her head straight? I felt I had failed at my job of being a mother; I should have been more forceful with Kirsty and insisted that she leave him, and maybe if I had she would be here now and none of us would be going through all this agony and heartache, and re-living it all again during this awful court case.

Every morning when I woke up I prayed that what I had been living through was a nightmare, and that when I got up my Kirsty would ring or text me and our lives could go back to the way they had been before. I just couldn't believe that she was gone, that she would never walk through the door again, that I would never see her or hear her voice again. I was in denial really, I guess it was a sort of coping mechanism. I was living on the edge as it was, I don't think I could allow myself to believe the pain and fear that my beautiful Kirsty had lived through.

In the months that followed I was tormented by images of Kirsty and fears that my daughter had still been alive when she was put into the suitcase. The pictures were like a video playing in a loop in my head, round and round, driving me insane. Unable to cope, seeing no way out of the nightmare that was driving me to madness.

Early one morning I got up, while Dave was still sleeping, and went to the cemetery; I took an overdose and lay down on Kirsty's grave, waiting to die. Back at home Dave woke up and realised I'd gone. Knowing how my mind was working he phoned the emergency services, and the police found me at the grave and took me to hospital where my stomach was pumped. Dave asked me to promise that I wouldn't do such a thing again and although all I wanted was to blot everything out forever, I did promise him. He didn't deserve to lose me too, and neither did Sonya and Hayley.

November arrived and with it came heavy rain and winds that caused flooding and damage in many parts of the country. It fitted my mood perfectly, and I was feeling grey and gloomy when the court case began. Sonya, Hayley, and Dave, were told to attend court, along with me, as we may have to be called as witnesses, but when we got there we were told that only I was going to be called and the other three weren't needed. I was annoyed because Sonya and Hayley had come all the way from Coventry to Swansea and it cost them time and money that they couldn't afford. Sonya also had to get someone to look after her children.

The police never apologised for this, even though they'd known for a couple of days that Sonya, Hayley, and Dave, were not needed and they hadn't let us know. I wasn't happy about that, and to be honest I started losing faith in the police, and kept thinking that if they carried on this way, then Grabham would walk away a free man.

When I saw Grabham in court that day I just stared at him again, but, this time, he never once looked my way. All he did was keep on yawning, the disrespectful bastard, and Sonya said to me, sarcastically, 'Aw look at him yawning Mum. We must be keeping him out of bed. Poor soul, he must be soo tired.' We just couldn't get over his behaviour, showing no respect at all.

We were then told that there was yet another delay and the trial would probably start properly after Christmas; all the police officers involved in the case said they hoped it wouldn't be on or near the anniversary of Kirsty's murder, because that would have been just awful for everyone. Luckily it wasn't; it started in the January 2010.

On a dark and wet Friday evening in November 2009 a couple of the policemen from the CID came to our house once again, saying they had news which they wanted us to hear before it was brought up in the trial. What on earth else could they have to tell us? Surely I'd heard and seen it all already. Whatever it was, it had to be more information confirming that Grabham was guilty.

One of them started talking, and indicated the couch. 'We want you to brace yourself for what we're going to tell you so you'd better sit down.' Dave and I sat, and waited.

It turned out that a computer expert had been going through Grabham's computer to see what he could find.

What he found was a website belonging to Grabham, advertising sex for sale. He was selling himself and Kirsty for sex, to both men and women. And the CID confirmed that Grabham and Kirsty had met in the massage parlour where they were both working as prostitutes. I'd already been told about the massage parlour, but the website was new. I felt myself become flushed, I was very angry. What had gone on with Grabham and my daughter?

Kirsty had always been such a good girl, I couldn't believe she would do what they were saying. But sadly, they had all the proof they needed, and more. On hearing this latest news, I loathed Grabham even more if it was possible.

I spoke to Kirsty's friend, Julie, about it all, and she told me everything she knew. Apparently when Kirsty started to work at the massage parlour the woman who ran it, the so-called madam, had a house available for rent, and she offered it to Kirsty. Kirsty was delighted and moved into the house, renting it for a very reasonable rate. Julie said that the madam used and abused all the girls working for her, and that Kirsty tried to leave several times, and each time, the madam told her she would be homeless and jobless if she didn't carry on working. Basically, she was blackmailing her. It was only when Kirsty got a flat from social housing that she was able to stop working in the massage parlour.

At least I had some kind of explanation for why she had worked at the massage parlour. I felt heartbroken for Kirsty, being put under such pressure. I wished that she had come to us, we would have helped her get away.

Julie told me that she wanted to tell me something, and that it would more than likely end in fisticuffs between her and the madam, but she didn't care as she felt that Dave and I were decent people and deserved the truth. But she said that as this would be our first Christmas without Kirsty, she would wait until afterwards to tell us because she didn't want to make it any worse for us. I wanted to know, but I agreed to wait another few weeks. I was sure it must be something I already knew, what more could there be, and what else could be worse than that?

The whole family usually enjoyed watching television in the run up to Christmas; all the series that had been running through the autumn were coming to an end and we always settled down for the finals, choosing our favourites to win whatever competition we were watching, but this year it all felt so flat. I knew that Kirsty would have liked Gino D'Acampo, who won I'm a Celebrity, not because he was a TV chef but because he was such a fun and lovable man. If I'm honest, I don't think Kirsty would've watched any cookery shows since she had no interesting in cooking whatsoever. I know she would have enjoyed seeing Joe McElderry win The X Factor; she always chose the young handsome ones! And she watched Strictly Come Dancing religiously because she loved the sparkly costumes and neat little shoes that the women wore, but I'm not sure she would have known who Chris Hollins was; he was the sports presenter who won it that year with his partner, Ola Jordan. Dave and I tried to get into the spirit of the season, but our hearts just weren't in it.

A couple of days before Christmas Julie rang and said she had a little guardian angel ornament for Kirsty, and she would bring it over on Christmas Eve morning so that we could put it on Kirsty's grave. I was looking forward to seeing her because I loved our conversations. Julie would tell me about some of the things she and Kirsty used to get up to and it made me so happy and so sad, both at the same time. We waited in for her all morning, but she never turned up. By one o'clock I was beginning to think maybe she had said she was coming on another day, not today, maybe I'd got the dates mixed up.

Then the phone rang and it was Julie's neighbour telling us that Julie was dead. 'What?' I cried, and passed the phone to Dave. I just couldn't believe it, poor Julie, only forty-four and mother to three lovely children, two boys and a girl. Julie's boyfriend, Gareth, came to see us a few days later, absolutely devastated. They found out that she had an undetected heart condition that had caused her death. He gave us the angel for Kirsty, and a Christmas card, and a small present for me from Julie, an ornamental glass oblong plaque. At the top it said what a special person I was, and underneath was a lovely poem. These things had been in Julie's handbag ready to give us on the day she was supposed to come and visit us. It was all so sad; Gareth had bought an engagement ring and had planned to propose to her on the Christmas Day.

I will never know what Julie was going to tell me. I sometimes wonder what it was, and I always say to people now, if you have something to say or do, do it today as tomorrow, as Julie has shown us, might never come.

Dave came with me to Julie's funeral, and the church, just as it had been with Kirsty, was packed to the rafters. Kirsty's death was still very raw, her funeral still fresh in my mind, and I felt overwhelmed with grief during the service. Julie was a very popular, much loved and respected woman. I went and kissed her coffin as I was leaving the church, and said my goodbyes to her. I couldn't believe she had gone, she was a true friend and one of the nicest people I had ever met, and I felt deeply sad that her life had ended so suddenly, just the same as my Kirsty's.

At this time we were still waiting for the trial to begin, and trying to get our heads around what we had been told about Grabham and Kirsty working in the sex industry; I knew Kirsty wouldn't do that of her own accord. I knew she was doing glamour modelling and doing very well at it. I hadn't been a hundred percent happy about the glamour modelling but told her to be careful about who she was working for and to stay safe; she travelled abroad a lot doing photography shoots and always showed me the photographs afterwards. They were lovely photos and not at all seedy as you'd imagine.

The time between the murder and the actual trial was awful for us; we just about got through each day as best we could, but Kirsty and Grabham were never far from our thoughts, both for different reasons, obviously. The fact that we would never ever see her or touch her again was and is the most difficult thing we've ever had to face up to. All that time we were trying to make sense of what had happened and what was happening to our close-knit family. I felt as if I had a heavy black shadow on my back that wouldn't let me move or function properly. How we got through those terrible depressing days only god knows. Once again the weather reflected our mood, freezing cold, snow and ice.

Just before the trial began, Grabham had to appear in court again, but this time he chose to go by video link rather than appear in person. 'Good', I thought, 'we must be getting to him at last.'

Chapter Six

The Trial

The trial was due to start on January 12, 2010 and it was estimated that it would last for about four weeks. In the end, it lasted just fifteen days, but those fifteen days seemed like fifteen years. We went to court on the first day to see the jury being chosen. There was a mixture of young and old people, and I remember looking at each and every one of them wondering if they would fall for Grabham's blatant lies, or would they see through him for the murdering scumbag that he was. I noticed a couple of young girls amongst them and prayed that he didn't charm them the way he had with my Kirsty and dozens of other young girls. After the judge was satisfied that none of them knew Kirsty or Grabham, or the massage parlour in Bridgend, they were all sworn in, and the trial was due to start the next day.

The media loved the whole sex trade, massage parlour, prostitute side of things and the newspaper headlines soon turned from 'Missing Model' to 'Murdered Prostitute'. That was how they were describing my daughter. For God's sake, she was dead! And she had a name – it was Kirsty. Not 'The Prostitute'. The press had no conscience, all they cared about was selling thousands more newspapers, making more money, regardless of the feelings of our family. People that we knew and lived near us said how disrespectful the press were being and that they should just drop it.

I loved my daughter regardless of what she was supposed to have done, she was still a human being and a victim in this awful nightmare. She was still my baby girl and she had never hurt anyone, only herself. Every time I read another vilifying headline about my daughter it was like a knife being pushed into my heart and being twisted full force.

I set up an RIP page on Facebook for Kirsty and within two days there were over three thousand messages of love and commiseration from family and friends. Some people referred to Kirsty as the family's 'Pink Princess', and the outpouring of warmth and respect, memories and sentiments, was wonderful.

My sisters came over one day to attend the trial; my sister Trisha had lost her husband, Ian, in November, just eight months after Kirsty died. He'd had a successful lung transplant and he was ready to come home but he needed a small biopsy; he had a major heart attack on the operating table and died. Trisha was heartbroken, but not long after he died she found some writing on his laptop. It was a message from Kirsty to me, and Trisha printed it out and brought it for me to read.

I DO NOT WANT YOU CRYING, I'M NOT SUFFERING ANY MORE.

I CAN SEE THINGS WILL GET BETTER, HIM YOU JUST IGNORE.

ITS TIME TO DRAW A LINE MUM, START TO OPEN THE DOOR,

I KNOW FOR YOU IT IS DIFFICULT, LOSING ME CAUSED PAIN

BUT HE WONT GET AWAY WITH IT, THEY HAVE GOT HIM INSANE,

I DON'T WANT YOU CRYING, I'M NOT SUFFERING
ANYMORE.

I KNOW WHAT YOU ARE THINKING, I VISIT YOU
EVERYDAY,

JUST KEEP ON SPEAKING SOFTLY I CAN HEAR
WHAT YOU SAY,

IF YOU LISTEN CAREFULLY, YOU'LL HEAR ME
RETURN YOUR PRAYER,

BE THINKING VERY POSITIVELY, WHEN GOING
UP THE STAIRS.

I'LL BE WATCHING YOU ALL FOR EVER, AND
PROTECTING DAY AND NIGHT,

YOU ARE NOW PROTECTED MOM WITH MY
RELIGIOUS LIGHT,

I'VE SPOKEN TO AUNTY TRISHA BY WAY OF
SPIRITUAL LINK,

AND I'VE SPOKEN TO AUNTY ISABELLA IN A
SIMILAR WAY THROUGH INK,

AND NOW I'M LINKED TO UNCLE IAN, WHO WILL
PUT INTO VERSE,

SO THAT YOU CAN UNDERSTAND, AND IT
DOESN'T FEEL ANY WORSE,

YOUR LOVE IS ALWAYS WITH ME, YOU SEND IT
EVERY DAY,

REMEMBER I'LL ALWAYS LOVE YOU, OF THAT
YOU CAN DEFINITELY SAY,

SO I DON'T WANT YOU CRYING, I'M NOT IN PAIN
ANYMORE.

MORE WORDS WILL COME BY POETRY, AND
SPIRITUAL MESSAGES TOO

AND WHEN YOU GET IN DIFFICULTY I WILL
GUIDE YOU THROUGH,

NO MORE CAN PEOPLE HURT ME, NO MORE CAN
THEY HURT YOU,

AS LONG AS WERE A FAMILY NO ONE CAN DRIVE
RIGHT THROUGH,

BELIEVE WE ARE TOGETHER, THAT NO ONE CAN
DISPEL.

AND IF THEY EVER TRIED IT, THEY'D BE SENT
RIGHT TO HELL.

The words had tears streaming down my cheeks, it was
just the kind of message I knew Kirsty would send me, kind
and loving and wanting me to be alright. I kept her message
close to me and re-read it often to give me strength.

I wasn't allowed into the courtroom until it was my turn
to testify, but Dave went in every day and he told me every
detail of what was happening, even though he wasn't supposed to. While I was hanging around waiting I happened
to look through a window into an office. In the corner I saw
a small black suitcase and I immediately knew it was the
one Kirsty had been stuffed into; it took my breath away
and made me feel sick to think my daughter had been put
into it when her little body was battered and still warm. I
rushed outside and went to a shop around the corner from
the courts and bought a half bottle of vodka and a bottle
of coke. I drank some of the vodka, and some of the coke,
straight from the bottles, then tipped the rest of the vodka
into the coke bottle, and walked slowly back to the court. I
sat on a bench outside the courtroom, drinking the mixture and tried to block out everything that was happening.

The moment I had been dreading for nearly a year
came on the third day. I was called to the witness stand.
All I remember is standing there visibly shaking, my legs
feeling as if they were going to buckle from under me. I

swore an oath on the bible and never once gave Grabham
the satisfaction of looking at him or acknowledging him, I
just looked directly at the jury. I think they could see the
pain and anguish of losing my child in my face, and I held
close to my heart the tiny pink knitted bonnet that Kirsty
had worn the first day I brought her home from hospital as
a baby.

Sonya came to court every day and stayed at our house
during the whole trial, but Hayley couldn't bear to go; she
couldn't bear to be in the same room as the man who had
so callously taken the life of her little Stig. She never once
attended court, she didn't want to see his face. She wanted
to get away from the whole thing and ended up going to
Istanbul for the length of the trial; why she did this I'll never
know, she never really spoke about it, just said she couldn't
bear to read and hear all the things that the press was writing about her little sister. The media had no idea how much
they were affecting my family with their sordid headlines.

It was only later I discovered that while she was away
Hayley had agreed to marry a Turkish man, to give him
British residency. If I had known what she was planning I'd
have strongly advised her not to do it, she was in a vulnerable state and no good would come of it. But in the end I
never did find out if she went ahead with it.

After I'd given my witness statement I was allowed into
the court to hear the rest of the trial. Three of the witnesses
were girls that Grabham had known since they were young;
they said he went to see them after killing Kirsty asking if
they'd be up for sex, and if not, would any of their friends be?
He hadn't seen these girls for many months, maybe years,
and he just turned up out of the blue asking for sex! One
thing that I noticed about these three girls was that they
were all petite and slim like Kirsty. Did Grabham purposely

pick small vulnerable girls so that he could control them? He'd even written a letter to one of these girls from jail; it was read out in court, and he told her he was missing his car and sex – 'You know what I am like.' I couldn't believe it. It wasn't even his car, it was Kirsty's. And he missed 'sex', not Kirsty. Imagine how I felt when I heard that. What a callous, cruel bastard.

Kirsty's bloodstained clothes were shown in court; there was so much blood. I can't and never will be able to describe how I felt that day, looking at those pieces of clothing, wondering which of her wounds the blood was from – her head where he tried to cave it in? Her back where he tried to cut her in half? My poor child, she must have bled so much. What kind of hell had she gone through that night? I still couldn't believe it.

At lunchtime that same day Grabham injured his ankle in a fall, whilst taking some exercise in the cell complex. The trial was adjourned until the next day, when he appeared using crutches. What a pity he hadn't broken his neck! One day I went to a toilet that I hadn't used before; it looked as if some work was being done in there because there were some broken tiles on the floor. I had an overwhelming desire to take a large piece of tile, hide it up my sleeve and, as Grabham went up to the witness box, rush over and destroy his ugly face with it. I wish now that I'd done that to him, then every time he looked in the mirror after that he would remember exactly why he was scarred.

A short DVD of the lounge in the flat was shown to the jury; the forensic scientist pointed out all the areas where Kirsty's blood was detected. There was blood everywhere, a wall near the entrance, splatters under a sofa, on the ceiling, on the television, the radiator, heavy staining on the sofa and the wall and on the taps and radiator in the bathroom. Attempts had been made to clean it all up and the ones on the ceiling had a fresh coat of paint over them. Despite being washed the jeans in the washing machine, Grabham's silver neck chain and his grey cardigan all had traces of blood on them.

A local shop where Grabham had bought the cleaning materials had him on CCTV buying the things, and the woman remembered him because he bought so much stuff, but despite the fact that he was caught on camera he claimed she was lying. The manager of La Tosca said he remembered Grabham and Kirsty in the bar on that last night; Grabham called him a liar. According to Grabham, every single person that stood in the witness box during the trial was a liar. All except him, of course. Even the most important witnesses, the young couple who lived in the flat below them, were branded as liars. They heard and saw Grabham stagger home on the night of the murder, they heard Kirsty arrive home and heard the noisy argument and Kirsty's high pitched screaming, followed by silence and then the sound of something being dragged across the floor – it was a laminated floor so they could hear everything. Then banging, drawers being opened and slammed, noises similar to someone searching for something. The arguments between Grabham and Kirsty were nothing new to the couple, so they hadn't thought it was anything unusual.

It made me sick to my stomach to think this poor young couple were describing to the jury just how my daughter was murdered. I wanted to shout at them to stop, I didn't want to hear anymore. For any parent to hear how their child died is just too awful for words. And the poor neighbours were really affected by Kirsty's murder and blamed themselves for not going upstairs that night to intervene, but how were they to know that this was different, or how dangerous

Grabham really was? It was nobody's fault except Grabham's, but it left them completely traumatised. Another couple of lives he's ruined. The young man looked across the court at Grabham and said 'I hope he rots in hell for what he did.'

Every day of the trial Dave and I and whatever family were there that day sat behind the witness box, but when it was Grabham's turn he started dictating to the court where he wanted us to sit – right up at the back on the other side of the witness box. Apparently, it was his 'human right'. Where were our human rights? As he hobbled past us to go into the box I felt like getting up and throttling him, but I decided he wasn't worth it, and anyway, why would I want to touch the vile scumbag who killed my daughter?

Asked if he had killed Kirsty, he said 'No'. Asked how Kirsty's blood was on his clothing he said, 'I don't know. I was asleep when she came in, and she was gone the next day.' He was trying to claim that while he was sleeping, someone else entered the flat, murdered Kirsty, went into the loft for the suitcase, stuffed her into it, cleaned up the blood, and then disposed of Kirsty's body in the case. Ha – and pigs might fly!

It came to light that at 9.30 am, just a few hours after killing Kirsty, Grabham set up a profile on a dogging website, looking for sex. He then went to the cashpoint and used Kirsty's debit card to get some money, and went to a brothel and paid some girl for sex. Kirsty wasn't even cold yet. To me he will always be a cold, psychopathic monster.

At the end of the trial when the judge reviewed the evidence and gave the jury his summing up, he told them they'd been introduced to a world of prostitution, brothels, drug taking, casual sex, and dogging sites on the internet, a world which they may have been unfamiliar with. But the jury weren't here to reach any sort of moral judgement about

Paul and Kirsty Grabham. 'This isn't a court of morals.' He
went on with the summing up of all the evidence the jury
had seen and heard, and then the jury went out to come up
with a decision as to whether Grabham was guilty or not.

All of the family were there and we were all bags of
nerves, sitting outside the courtroom, hoping and praying
that the result would be the correct one and that Grabham
would be found guilty. For the first time in my life I bit my
nails right down to the skin. I kept imagining Grabham
walking out a free man. Did he fool the jury, would they fall
for his evil lies? The jury returned after three and a quarter
hours and hadn't reached a verdict. I was shocked – how
could they not see that he was guilty, that he was the only
one who could have murdered my daughter? It was late and
we were told to come back the next day. I didn't know if my
nerves were up to it.

The following day the jury were out for six hours discuss-
ing the case. By the time we were called back into the courtroom for the verdict we were in bits. Family and friends and
the press were all squeezed into the small courtroom; it was
standing room only as the foreman of the jury was asked to
stand and deliver the verdict. When he said 'Guilty' it was as
if a weight had been lifted from me, and the silent tension
was broken by a loud cheer from the public gallery. The
judge threatened to clear the court if it happened again,
but later he offered his condolences to us, Kirsty's family,
and said that this had been a terrible ordeal for us and
apart from one understandable outburst we had behaved
with great dignity. We were over the moon, so relieved and
happy that the right decision had been made.

The judge then spoke to Grabham, describing the
despicable things he had done to Kirsty; "I have watched
throughout this trial for the merest flicker of remorse in

your eyes and I have seen none," he told him. He added: "You have been convicted of murder – just one year after you promised to love and cherish your new bride, you battered and strangled her to death. It was a vicious and sustained attack fuelled by drink and drugs that you had taken and it is without doubt that your intention was to kill her. But she was not to have, even in death, the decency and dignity to which, undoubtedly, she was entitled. You crammed her bleeding and still warm body into a suitcase like so much rubbish, hoping it would not be found for many years."

He said that his conduct could only be described as cold, callous, calculating, and utterly selfish, conduct that gravely aggravated the already serious nature of the offence. He emphasized that the term to be served was not trying to place a value on Kirsty's life, which was priceless. The starting point for murder was fifteen years, but he was increasing it to nineteen years to take account of his behaviour after the murder, pretending that she was still alive when he knew all along that she was dead. I never once glanced at Grabham as all this was said. I was sad, but elated at the same time.

Nineteen years for killing my beloved daughter was not long enough though, a life for a life is what I believe in; take a life, then serve a life, that is what should happen to murderers like him. I wasn't really happy with the sentence and truly believed he should have got more, but no matter how long he is locked up for it will never bring my Kirsty back.

For the first two or three years after Kirsty's murder I wanted Grabham tortured and dead, I wanted him to really hurt, but now I want him to do his bloody nineteen years and then to be executed. I want him to suffer as my family and I have suffered, then let me, and a lot of other parents who have lost a child in the same way as I have, get him in a room and let us spend an hour or so with him and see how he likes it.

After the judge finished his summing up and passed sentence on Grabham we all traipsed out of the courtroom and into a side room. The police gave us a Victim Impact Statement to read out to the press. Sonya bravely said that she would read it. My sister Isabella had written the original statement for us but the police said we weren't allowed to read it because we told the truth about how the press had treated us. I told Emma Hughes, the PFLO, that the press couldn't hurt us any more so why couldn't we read it? She said we'd be surprised at what the press can do. The judge had read it, but I wasn't happy that it wasn't read out in court. Maybe it was because I'd christened the press The Enemy.

Outside the court there were so many more people from the media than I'd expected; Sonya spoke to them, reading the statement that the police had written for us. In it she mentions that the day Kirsty died our hearts died with her and that we never had the chance to say goodbye. That the sentence passed on Paul Grabham is nothing compared to the life sentence imposed on us and that our lives are no longer complete without our pink princess. She said that the last time we saw Kirsty she had been battered almost beyond recognition, and that memory will live with us forever, that her battered face is the last thing we see before we fall asleep at night, and the first thing we see when we wake up in the morning. She thanked everyone involved in putting Grabham behind bars and for all the support we'd received from family and friends. She said that all Kirsty ever wanted to be was to be loved and to be a mother. And then I read out a poem that the police had found in Kirsty's journal and had given to me. It was called, My Mum.

'A mum is god's love in action.
She looks with her heart and feels with her eyes.
A mum is a bank where her children deposit all their worries
and hurt.
A mum is the cement that keeps her family together and Her love
lasts a lifetime.'

Underneath this Kirsty had written "I love you lots and lots, you are the best mum ever. I don't tell you often enough but believe me you truly are. Love Kirsty.' That really broke my heart.

We invited the police officers, CID, and everyone else involved in Kirsty's murder trial to come over to the pub across the road for a celebratory drink. We'd been in there for about half an hour when there was a loud shout saying that the security van that Grabham was in was about ready to leave the courtyard. Everyone ran out of the pub and across the road, bringing traffic to a halt, and ran towards the van just as they were opening the big gates from the courthouse parking area. The officer opening the gates looked at us and said 'He's sitting in the front, on the right-hand side.' Well, we started hitting the windows of the van with our fists and handbags, screaming at Grabham, 'Die you evil bastard, die, burn in hell.' One of my friends even crouched down in front of the van pretending to do up the laces on her trainers, giving us more time to scream and shout at the monster inside.

After Kirsty died one of her friends adopted her little cat, her beloved Princess; on the day that Grabham received his sentence that cat managed to escape from the house and the garden, and got run over and killed by a car. I just thought it was strange that Princess joined Kirsty on this particular day. Maybe she was waiting for justice to be done before going to join her mum.

CHAPTER SEVEN
AFTER THE TRIAL

Things settled down after the trial, but I still had some questions. Firstly, how did Grabham get Kirsty's dead body down all those concrete stairs, in that suitcase, on his own? It was either adrenaline, or he had help from another person. And where did her pink hair straighteners disappear to? I believe these were the weapon used to cave Kirsty's head in, and he had thrown them away somewhere. I don't think he'd have said they were missing unless he'd used them in the murder and wanted to throw the scent off. Julie Thomas had always said she would love to search every inch of the side of the M4 looking for those straighteners, she and I were both convinced they were the murder weapon. I know I will never get the answers to these questions; the only ones who know the truth are Grabham, who is never going to tell us, and Kirsty.

I still sometimes expected Kirsty to be on the other end of the phone when it rang, or to be coming in the front door when I heard it open. Sometimes, on the street, I'd see someone that I thought was Kirsty and I'd rush over and grab her arm, only for a stranger to turn and look at me.

At the funeral, I had put a photograph of Kirsty on her coffin, and afterwards I kept it in my handbag so that she was always with me. Several times I got it into my head that she was still alive, still missing, and I would go around the town with that photo, showing it to people and asking if they'd seen her. They would shake their heads sadly and give me a sympathetic look, knowing who I was because of the headline newspaper and television reports that they'd seen during the trial.

It was another month or so before we were allowed into Kirsty's flat. Two police officers came to our house and drove me, with Sonya and our friend Beverly, (the mother of Kirsty's lovely ex-boyfriend Jonny), the half hour or so to Swansea. I remember thinking that it was no wonder Kirsty was so slim, having to trudge up these concrete stairs day in and day out. But as we approached the door I suddenly felt like running away; this was where my daughter's brutal murder had taken place and I really didn't know if I could face going in.

But I did, I took a deep breath and stepped through the door. I was shocked to see hundreds of green arrows stuck all over the walls and ceiling, they were even on the television and the wardrobe in the bedroom, all pointing to splashes of blood. Oh, my god, it was so much worse than I'd imagined. It looked as if it had been raining blood. When I went into the bedroom and opened the wardrobe I saw a track suit top and a pair of jeans hanging up; holding them to my nose I inhaled deeply. Kirsty's smell was still on the clothes; I buried my face in the fabric and memories flooded through my mind, so many memories. It was only then that I broke down and started sobbing. And once I started I couldn't stop.

We packed up Kirsty's clothes, many that she never lived to wear because they still had the labels on. We had to work quickly, me with tears running down my cheeks, because we only had three days to empty the flat, so we did what we could in such a short space of time. The forensics and police had trashed the flat, it was such a mess we didn't even know where to begin clearing it out. We kept a lot of Kirsty's clothes and shoes for Hayley because they were the same size, and we gave the rest to charity. Anything of Grabham's got spat on and put in the rubbish bags. I noticed there were no towels anywhere, and I could only guess Grabham had used them to clean up Kirsty's blood.

It was a terrible ordeal, clearing out my murdered daughter's flat. I kept picturing her poor body lying where forensics thought she'd been lying when Grabham struck her; I shuddered, moved away, and tried to focus on something else, anything to stop me thinking and picturing what Kirsty had been through. My heart was like lead, and there was a lump in my throat that made it difficult to swallow. I was glad when we'd finally finished.

A couple of months later the CID gave us four bags of Kirsty's belongings that they'd taken from the flat for the trial, and they also returned her car. Yes, the car that Grabham had put my Kirsty's poor broken body in after he murdered her; the car Grabham used to have sex with other women. I didn't want it sitting on my drive, so a friend took it and sold it for me. The buyer knew the history but was okay with it.

Amongst the things the CID gave me were Kirsty's journals. It made me so sad reading them, it broke my heart to learn that Kirsty was too scared of Grabham to leave him, and dreaded him coming home, wondering what he was going to do to her. I wondered why this hadn't been read out in court, it was clear evidence that she was terrified of him.

A few months later Dave and I were in Swansea; we had been walking round town for a while when decided to sit on a bench for a little rest. A gentleman walked over to us and asked if we were Kirsty's parents. When we confirmed that we were, he told us he'd been on the jury at her trial. He said it was one of the toughest, most harrowing things he'd been through in his life and all of the jurors were crying in the jury room, they were so upset. I asked him if all of the jury thought Grabham was guilty and he said there were two that questioned his guilt, and when I asked him if the two were older people, he said no, it was the two young girls. I bloody knew it! Grabham had somehow charmed the young ones from the dock in the courtroom. But this gentleman said everyone else could see he was guilty, it was so blatantly obvious that there shouldn't have been the need for a trial, Grabham should have been locked up and the key thrown away. I thanked him for making the right decision, and he walked away with his head bowed.

In October 2010 Sonia Oatley's sixteen-year-old daughter, Rebecca, was murdered by her boyfriend, Joshua Davies, when he lured her to woods and hit her over the head with a rock the size of a rugby ball. A year later the judge sentenced Davies to a minimum of fourteen years. This happened in Bridgend, just around the corner from me and, knowing what Sonia was going through, I got in touch to offer any support or help that I could.

We were both outraged at the length of the sentences that both Grabham and Davies had been given, nineteen and fourteen years; they will both still be young men when they are released and they can go on to have full lives. We firmly believe that a life sentence should be for life, not for fourteen years, or nineteen years, but for the rest of the killer's natural life.

Sonia Oatley and I joined together calling for tougher sentences for killers. We wrote to the Home Secretary and to the Prime Minister to appeal for a review of the judicial system in the United Kingdom, for life tariffs to mean exactly that – Life. We did have a petition online for several years, and we managed to get interviews in the newspapers, but the campaign ran out of steam and eventually the petition got taken down.

I will never get over the ordeal of losing my beloved child; I think of her constantly with love and pride. She was and always will be, my pink princess. And when she died I thought that losing a child was the most awful thing any parent could go through. But I was wrong. Losing two children was the most dreadful experience that any parent could go through – as I was about to find out.

CHAPTER EIGHT
HAYLEY

Hayley didn't leave Istanbul until she was sure the media circus surrounding the trial had disappeared. I spoke to her on the phone and texted her every other day, but she refused to talk about Kirsty. Whenever I mentioned her little sister, Hayley would change the subject. I think it was so painful for her that she had to seal it in a box in her heart and never open it up again.

I believe she started drinking heavily to stop her mind from dwelling on Kirsty because thinking about her little sister, her Stig, was unbearable for her. I'm just grateful that she didn't come to the mortuary because if she had, the image of Kirsty's battered face would have burned itself into her brain, as it had mine. Hayley wouldn't have been able to deal with that at all, goodness knows what she might have done.

Hayley came to visit us every few weeks, although she never went back to see Kirsty's grave. She seemed to be drinking more each time she came and she didn't appear to be eating very much and as time wore on I thought she looked worse and worse. I became very worried about her, and I sat her down and told her she would have to stop drinking or she would end up where her little sister was. She ignored my reference to Kirsty and promised she would start eating properly and stop drinking so much. While she was visiting she did try, but as soon as she was back in Coventry she went back to her old habits. I could hear it in her voice when we talked on the phone, even though she denied it.

At one time, I persuaded her to come and stay with Dave and me, and I managed to keep her with us for six weeks. I made sure she ate every meal I put in front of her and tried to make her stop drinking and after the six weeks she was looking and feeling much healthier. I took her to get her hair done and she looked absolutely amazing; her skin was clear, her eyes were bright, and she looked almost as gorgeous as she did before the drink took hold.

She returned to Coventry and I hoped she would eat properly and stay off the drink, but she was soon back to her old life and her old ways; she just seemed to fall apart again when she was on her own. It was as if she couldn't manage or think for herself and needed someone to tell her when to do things, even everyday things such as taking a shower and brushing her teeth. I begged her to move back to South Wales and let me look after her but she wouldn't hear of it.

She eventually became very ill, she was poisoning herself with alcohol and she was in and out of hospital with low potassium and sodium, which probably led to her heart problems; her heart stopped on numerous occasions and she had to have it restarted. I remember her telling me that one time her heart had stopped for twenty seconds, and now, anytime I'm using my microwave and it starts to count down from twenty seconds, I have to look away because it reminds me of Hayley's heart stopping.

I worried about her every day, and every time the phone rang I thought it would be someone ringing to tell me she was dead. I told her this but she just told me not to worry, that she would be okay. Hayley marched to her own tune, she always had, and nobody could tell her what to do. I told her that I would never stop worrying about her, she was my little girl and I would worry about her until the day I died. Sadly, she beat me to it.

One time when she was visiting, about eighteen months after the trial, she told me there was a lump in her vagina. She was obviously worried about it so I took her to my GP and even went into the consulting room with her to make sure she told the doctor about it. He gave her some antibiotics, which initially cleared it up, but she told me a month or so later that it had come back again and promised she would go to her own GP in Coventry, which she did. She was referred to the hospital and they decided to operate to remove it and a date was set for November. I was going to go to Coventry to be with her and look after her, but she said not to, that it was such a minor operation that she'd be in and out on the same day.

On the day of the operation I was on tenterhooks, waiting for Hayley to get home from the hospital and give me a ring to let me know she was alright. But when the phone did ring, it was the hospital calling to tell me to get over there as soon as possible, that Hayley was on a life support machine. I was so shocked that I didn't think to ask any questions. Dave and I just phoned for a cab, rushed to the station to get the train to Coventry and then got a taxi to the hospital as quickly as we could, praying that she would be okay. How could she be on the verge of death when she only went in for a minor operation?

When we got to intensive care I was horrified. There was my Hayley lying flat on the bed with all these machines bleeping, and tubes and wires all over her body. It reminded me of a giant ball of string with no beginning and no end.

I'm not a religious person but, believe me, that day I prayed with all my heart that Hayley would pull through.

The doctor heard we had arrived and took us into a side room. He said Hayley was seriously ill and that it was highly unlikely she would pull through; she had pneumonia and sepsis. I asked him what had happened, as she'd only gone in for a routine operation. He told me the operation was cancelled because there was an emergency they had to deal with, but the lump on her vagina, which was more of a blister, had burst and caused the sepsis. He explained that sepsis is a life-threatening condition that arises when the body's response to an infection injures its own tissues and organs, and can lead to shock, multiple organ failure and death, especially if not recognized early and treated promptly.

I was numb, I couldn't believe this was happening. 'Please doctor, please save her, I'm begging you,' I cried. 'You've caught it early and treated it quickly so you've got to save her. I've not long ago lost her little sister to murder. I can't bear to lose another child. If she goes too I think I'll just shrivel up and die.'

The doctor looked really sad and said he would try his best, 'But you need to prepare for the worst. Even though we're treating it aggressively only a miracle can save her now I'm afraid.'

I spent as long as I could sitting at Hayley's bedside, praying that she would survive, and when I got so tired that I could hardly see straight I went to Sonya's house to get a few hours' sleep. I was just out of the shower and getting ready to go back to sit by Hayley's bedside when a call came from the hospital. My heart sank as I took the phone from Sonya's hand. The doctor that I'd spoken to the day before was on the other end of the line and he started right in as soon as I'd said 'Hello.'

'Do you remember the conversation yesterday when I said that only a miracle can save your daughter? Well that miracle has happened. We'll be taking Hayley off the life support machine shortly to see if she can breathe on her own.'

You can imagine the joy, the elation, that flooded my body, and I almost flew to the hospital and in to see Hayley. It was such a great feeling to see her breathing on her own, it truly was a miracle. I am sure, even to this day, that Kirsty was looking down on Hayley and protecting her; she didn't want her older sister to join her – after all, she didn't want Hayley going up to heaven and stealing her thunder, not just yet.

I sat by Hayley's bed, stroking her hand, and told her that when she was better Dave and I would take her on holiday somewhere warm. When she was discharged from the hospital she was very weak, and still wouldn't eat. But a couple of months later, in January, she was strong enough to go on holiday, so we took her to Tunisia for a week. I will always remember that holiday with great fondness; we had a lovely time, the Tunisian people were so friendly and helpful and the weather was sunny and warm but even so, I noticed Hayley was still drinking far more than she should have been.

I was shocked to realise that she had a drink on her bedside table to wake up to, and I also noticed that when she did manage to eat a small amount of food she would go to the toilet straight away; I just knew she was making herself sick. When I challenged her about it she denied it, but I knew in my heart that she had some kind of eating disorder; maybe it was part of being an alcoholic, I didn't know. I reminded her that Kirsty was looking down on her and didn't want her up there, that a place in heaven wasn't ready for her just yet. She laughed and said, 'Don't you worry, that old grim reaper isn't getting his hands on me just yet.'

We all thought that Hayley would give up the alcohol after what happened to her in the hospital. We believed that being put on a life support machine would have shocked her so much that she would stop drinking, but sadly the drink, the enemy, was the winner.

About this time, Hayley met a chap named Jamie on the internet; he was from Doncaster, and he moved down to live with her in Coventry. The trouble was, Jamie was an alcoholic as well and of course that was not good for Hayley; he was just a drinking partner for her. During the year that they were together she was in and out of hospital more than twenty times.

In June 2014 Dave and I had a party to celebrate what would have been Kirsty's thirtieth birthday. Hayley and Jamie both came and stayed with us for a few days and Hayley was in a right mess. Apart from her clothes looking grubby and wrinkled, she appeared bloated and tired, could hardly move, and when she walked she shuffled like an old lady. Even getting upstairs was difficult for her and I was shocked to see that she had to crawl up on her hands and knees. She didn't eat a thing while she was with us and, thinking I could shock her, I asked if I could phone The Jeremy Kyle show and try to get her into some kind of rehab; she didn't get it though, she just said she would be too embarrassed to go on television. I told her it would be better to be embarrassed than dead, that the answer wasn't in the bottom of a bottle. I'd found that out myself after Kirsty's murder, when I found myself drinking quite heavily to blot it all out.

The day after the party, on the Sunday, I had to call an ambulance for Hayley; she started off in the morning feeling very ill, but then she began having seizures. I was completely shocked to see my daughter like that; she looked deformed and she was so stiff she couldn't move any part of her body, it was locked in one position, but at the same time her whole body was shuddering and convulsing; her teeth were clenched, then foam started coming out of her mouth. I thought she was going to die there and then and I was sick with fear. My heart was hammering, and I was sweating and shaking with dread.

She was in the hospital for six days that time but she signed herself out of the hospital the following Saturday, and when she and Jamie came back to our house I could smell alcohol on both of them. They had gone to the pub on the way home from the hospital! I couldn't believe it, I was so angry I just screamed at Hayley, 'You're going to die if you don't stop this drinking and not eating. How can you be so reckless? Both of you!'

Hayley said they'd only had one glass of wine each but I knew that this was a lie, I knew they had drunk more than that. I went mental at them, 'How can you be so stupid as to go on drinking after the scare we all got? Have you forgotten you nearly died, that you were on a life support machine just a few months ago?'

'Oh Mum, every conversation we have is about my drinking and eating. You're starting to sound like a broken record. I've told you, I know what I'm doing and I'm going to be okay.'

Then I turned on Jamie and asked him why he let her go to the pub, and all he would say was, 'Well, I wasn't going to let her go on her own, I wasn't going to desert her.'

They were both unhappy about my harsh words, but I only spoke the truth; I had already lost one daughter and I didn't want to lose Hayley. I couldn't stand the thought of burying another daughter.

That afternoon they left without saying a word to me and got the train back to their flat in Coventry. After they had gone I went in to clean the bedroom they'd been sleeping in and found empty booze bottles everywhere; under the pillow, under the bed, even in carrier bags in a drawer of the dressing table.

On October 6, Sonya decided to call in and see Hayley. She was totally shocked and scared by what she found. Hayley was lying on the settee, extremely ill; she could hardly move, her stomach was bloated so much that she looked heavily pregnant, and her skin and the whites of her eyes were pure yellow. Sonya rang Hayley's doctor, who told her to call an ambulance right away. Once again Hayley was taken to hospital, and she said to Sonya 'I feel like I am going to die.'

I phoned the hospital every day to see how she was, and they always said she was stable. When I rang on the Thursday, October 9, I was told she was on the 'good side of ten', and I was really happy. I thought she would be home in no time, just the same as all the other times she'd been in hospital, but when I phoned the next day I was told that she'd taken a turn for the worse during the night and to get there as soon as I could, that she was very ill and had been rushed into intensive care.

I panicked, of course; my stomach was doing somersaults thinking that Hayley might die before we got there. It was déjà vu, an action replay of the last time, getting a taxi to the station, a train to Coventry, and another taxi to the hospital at the other end. It seemed to take forever to get there and for the whole journey from South Wales to Coventry I was praying that Hayley would still be alive, because the last time I spoke to her we argued about her drinking. I needed her to be alive to tell her how much I loved her, and kept repeating to myself, over and over and over, 'Please let her be alive when we get there. Please let her be alive when we get there.'

As we hurried towards intensive care Sonya, and Hayley's partner Jamie, were just coming out from seeing her and walking along the corridor towards us. I immediately saw red; I punched Jamie, and screamed in his face, 'This is your fault, all your fault that Hayley is in there. You should be looking after her, but you're the one going to the shop and buying the drink for her. It's all your fault!', and I rushed into the room to Hayley's bedside.

When I saw Hayley, I was so shocked at the state of her that I burst into tears. I just couldn't stop crying and thinking to myself that this was it, we are going to lose her. Then I remembered back to when she'd been on the life support machine and had survived, and I convinced myself that she would survive again. My thinking was very mixed up.

A nurse came and told me the doctor wanted to speak to me, and took me to the same little side room that I'd been in before. A doctor was sitting on one of the chairs and a nurse was standing beside him, and he told me bluntly, 'Hayley isn't going to see tomorrow; she will be dead. All her vital organs are shutting down.'

I sank to my knees, crying and begging, 'Please, please it's not true. Please try and save her, I don't want to lose my little girl. I've already lost one child, please don't let me lose another.' I don't know if I was begging the doctor, or God, because I was on my knees in front of the doctor, with my hands together, praying. 'Please save her.'

The nurse helped me to my feet as the doctor spoke. 'The next twenty-four hours will be crucial.' He didn't mean it though, he knew Hayley wouldn't survive that long; it was just to give me a little bit of hope to cling to, and time to let it sink in that Hayley couldn't be saved this time.

I composed myself before going back to Hayley's bedside, and I told her I loved her. She said, 'Love you too, Mum.' And they were the sweetest words my ears had ever heard. She told Sonya she loved her too; she knew she wasn't going to recover this time. All my sisters came to the hospital to support me, and to say goodbye to Hayley; it was just so sad. When they left, Hayley said to a nurse, 'Hold hands,' and the nurse said, 'Do you want to hold my hand?', and Hayley said 'No, my mums'. She knew she was going to heaven, to be with her little Stig.

I sat down on a hard chair next to the bed and held her hand for hours, I didn't want to let it go. I was trying to read a book but the words were just a blur and I kept reading the same paragraph over and over again. I couldn't concentrate, but I was trying not to think about the fact that Hayley would be gone soon, up to heaven to be reunited with her little sister. I was trying my best to just have this precious time alone with my girl.

Dave and Sonya went into a room that was kept for family members of very ill patients, and tried to get a little sleep, but they were both back in the ward within the hour. They couldn't sleep, they were too worried and concerned about Hayley. I just sat there speaking to Hayley. I didn't know if she could hear me, she was slipping away, but they say that hearing is the last sense to go, and I still hoped that if I kept on speaking to her she might just hear me and get better.

I talked to her about some of the holidays we'd had, happy ones, such as the time we went to Florida and we lost Kirsty in one of those massive theme parks. We found her after ten minutes coming out of a shop, wearing a Davey Crocket hat and munching on a bag of sweets. It wasn't funny at the time, I was furious, but years later we often spoke about it and we had a good old laugh. And I talked about the camping holiday we'd had in the peak district, it was a cheap and cheerful holiday but we loved it, the scenery was beautiful and the novelty of camping was just something else.

I reminded her about the little Jack Russell dog we had, called Gnasher, she was a lovely dog and funny, and we all loved her. Sadly, she was bitten by a rat near my father's house and caught an infection so we had to have her put down, but while she was with us Gnasher brought us a lot of happiness. I continued talking to her about whatever came to my mind, about Kirsty, about me and Dave, about Sonya and her gorgeous children, even about Harry Potter, until the doctor came a few hours later.

He asked me to think about switching off the machines that were keeping Hayley alive; he said they were only there for the family's sake and it would be kinder to let her go. He said if it was a member of his family he would turn them off.

How can a parent make a decision like that? How could he even think of asking me to turn off the machines that were keeping my beautiful, much loved, daughter alive? I begged him to let me try and make her better, told him she could have one of my kidneys and my liver, all of my organs, but please, not to let her die. Like any other mum I would have given my life for my child; I had lived my life but Hayley had not. I climbed onto the bed beside her and tried to give her a cuddle.

The doctor said he would let the registrar make the decision when to turn off the machines, and then the decision to end Hayley's life would not be down to me. I agreed, but asked if we could have her footprints and handprint taken first, because I wanted them done while she was still alive, and I watched as the nurse did it for me. I also wanted a lock of her lovely long hair, the hair that she was so proud of, and as the nurse began cutting the hair, Hayley made a rasping noise.

'Oh, she's telling you off for cutting her hair.' I said with a little smile, thinking of the times when she was younger that she would laughingly 'tell me off' for silly things. Little did I know that this was the death rattle. Hayley then gave two small sighs, the last physical sign of her life, and stopped breathing. It was one minute past five in the morning. When the nurse told me she was gone, I said, 'How do you know?' The nurse pointed to the machine that was monitoring Hayley's heartbeat, and it had a zero on it.

That was it. Hayley was dead. Gone as quickly as that. I had held her in my arms as she took her last breath. She was no age at all, only thirty-one years old. I began to cry as it sank in, I couldn't believe it, my Hayley was gone. It hurt so much I felt as if a huge hand had reached into my chest and ripped my heart out through my ribs. I thought I was going to collapse, or die even. The nurse suggested that we wait outside while they got Hayley settled and removed all the tubes, wires, and monitors from her.

The three of us, Dave, and Sonya, and I, walked out to the corridor, shocked and in tears. Surely we were dreaming and this couldn't be real? When we were allowed back into the ward, all the paraphernalia was gone from Hayley, and the nurse had brushed Hayley's hair, and teeth, and put the comfort blanket on that Hayley had taken into hospital with her. She just looked like she was asleep, 'my sleeping beauty' I thought. I held her hands as tears rolled down my cheeks; my poor baby was gone. I would never see her beautiful face or hear her infectious giggle ever again.

What had I done in life that was so bad, so terrible, that I deserved this? To lose one child was bad enough, but to lose two was totally against all odds. Unbelievable! Never again would we be a complete family; two precious links were missing from the family chain, Hayley and Kirsty. That old Grim Reaper, as Hayley had called death, had come and taken her away like a thief in the night. He had won. Hayley was gone. I just hoped to god that Kirsty and all of my dear departed loved ones would be waiting for Hayley to show her the way.

Dave and I would be staying with my sister, Trisha, until after the funeral, and she was waiting for us, stunned. Trisha advised us to use the same funeral director that she had used for her husband Ian a few years earlier. I knew this was a hard task for her, but she showed such strength and courage; she drove us there, and sat in the same room with us where she'd sat not long before, making her husband's funeral arrangements.

I had pleaded with the hospital not to cut up Hayley's body, but to leave it intact; thankfully they agreed to my wishes so there was no need to wait and Hayley could be collected whenever we could arrange it. I wanted the funeral director to get Hayley's body from that horrible cold mortuary straight away; I didn't want her lying around for weeks the way her little sister Kirsty had. I wanted her funeral over and done with as soon as possible.

I was living in a dazed nightmarish state; I felt this horrible thing must be happening to someone else, not to me. Surely I would wake up soon. Sadly, that wasn't to be. When I went to bed with Dave at night we clung to each other, crying our hearts out, overcome with grief and pain. We found it difficult to sleep, and each morning we had to find a backbone and legs to even get out of the bed. But I had to get up and get on with it, there was a funeral to arrange.

We were seriously beginning to wonder if the family was cursed; ever since we lost Kirsty it seemed we'd had nothing but bad luck. Trisha had lost her husband Ian, another sister Maggy found a lump on her foot and went to the doctors. It turned out to be a cancerous growth and she had to have half of her leg amputated. And now Hayley was gone. I remember looking up at the sky and screaming 'What else are you going to throw at us? Come on, give it your best shot.'

Trisha drove us to Hayley's flat so that we could clear out as much of her stuff as we could. My other sister Isabella met us outside; she is very spiritual, and when she arrived she told me she'd received a message from Hayley. She'd written it down. It said:

'Hello Mum, I am fine and I was happy to come here. It is a lovely place and I am with Kirsty and Sailor [my father]. We are all happy to be together again. I was not happy when I was on the earth plane and I always wanted to leave it. But I love you and daddy Dave and I want you to be smiling when I look at you, and don't cry because I am fine now and I am happy. I am not in any pain and I love where I am. When I came here I was so surprised, it is a beautiful place and I am happy to be here. Take care of my man for me. Tell him to be happy and stop all the drinking, there isn't an answer to a problem at the bottom of a bottle. I was silly at times to do what I done but I was unhappy in my soul. I couldn't talk about what I felt and I struggled all the time. But I am all right now and those days are best forgotten. I love you my little Mummy, I will be with you all the time and I will let you know when I am around. And you better watch out, because now me and Kirsty are back together again there will be trouble in heaven. We are happy mummy, and we love you both. We will be with you always.'

This message did bring me and Dave some comfort. It helped to think of my girls together and up to their old tricks.

Packing up Hayley's things I noticed that most of the clothes she had were ones I had given her; she must never have bought any for herself. I suppose nothing was as important as the booze, not clothes, not food, not even family. There was alcohol everywhere, and a good amount of food in the fridge, so someone was buying the food but she hadn't been eating it. Jamie just sat there drinking cider while we packed up and cleared things around him. He was really making me angry and I wanted to shake him and tell him to move his ass and help us sort out Hayley's belongings. And to stop drinking – couldn't he see that he would end up like Hayley if he didn't stop?

On the morning of the funeral we went to see Hayley in her coffin at the funeral parlour. She still looked very bloated, and so sad; she was wearing a lilac sheath which was very pretty, but the empty body wasn't my Hayley, it looked like someone else completely and so sad. I remember looking at her nose and in her left nostril was a few drops of blood, so I wiped it with a tissue. I still have that tissue, it's a little bit of Hayley.

I had asked everyone to wear something lilac or purple to the funeral if they were able, and most people did; they were Hayley's favourite colours. A lot of my old friends came along, some that I hadn't seen in years; I was so grateful that they turned up to help me lay my daughter to rest.

We had lost touch with Hayley's daughter, Megan Eve, because her other grandmother and her partner Eric, had moved about six years earlier and hadn't told us where they were moving, so Hayley had lost all contact with her daughter. But she never stopped looking for her, she even phoned the police and social services to ask how she could find her, but nobody could help her. We knew Megan Eve was better off with her other grandparents but it would have been nice to keep in touch with her.

Just on the off chance, my son in law, John, phoned the last pub they had managed, hoping we could get in touch with Megan Eve. Luckily the new landlord knew them and promised to let them know that Hayley had died. Sue then phoned John and he gave her all the details.

Megan Eve said she wanted to come to the funeral, and when I saw her I got such a big lump in my throat. At 13 I couldn't believe how big she had grown and how much she resembled her mother. She was just gorgeous. She had a big arrangement of beautiful flowers, and she took some of the white roses out and placed them on Hayley's coffin; they were the only flowers there and it was so lovely to know they were from her little girl. I just hoped that Hayley was looking down and could see that Megan Eve was there. She sat next to me during the service and, bless her, she cried her little heart out. I held her hand and thought my heart would burst with sadness. I know she could never have had a relationship with her mom, but I wish Hayley had got to see her before she passed away.

One of Hayley's best friends, Leanne Collins, wrote out a few precious memories and read them out during the service and it made me smile to think of the mischief they had got up to. Megan Eve and Anais, Sonya's eldest daughter, had made a lovely collage with pictures of Hayley on it and they had it at the wake. It was lovely.

Later, in a pub, everyone was laughing, joking, and being happy, all very normal in a pub, but I couldn't stand it and started screaming at them to shut up. 'Don't you realise my little girl is gone and she's never coming back? If I can't be happy how dare you be happy?' I slumped into my seat and sobbed. I was lucky that everyone knew I was a bereaved mother who had just said goodbye forever to her second child, and that I didn't mean to be horrible.

We had Hayley cremated so that I could take her home to South Wales with me. The days after her death are all just one blur, but I have learned to cope just a little bit better. I feel like I have lost my heart and soul. It is a struggle to get up each day and I have no life in me. I am soulless. I often sit around in my night clothes all day. My life is ruined. If it wasn't for Sonya and my grandchildren I know I wouldn't be here; they are what keep me from taking my own life.

My three girls got on really well, hardly ever arguing, and when they did argue it was over something trivial. Kirsty's murder devastated Sonya, and she had to have counselling, as did her daughter Anais, when she was only 8 years old. Whenever Sonya and I speak on the phone, which is often, the conversation always works its way round to the deaths of Kirsty and Hayley.

Sometimes people ask me how I carry on and say that I must be a very strong woman. But I am not strong, I am weak. I don't want to carry on with this heartache, but I have to for the sake of all my loved ones still here. I have my lovely brave beautiful daughter, Sonya, and her children, my grandchildren, Anais, Amelia, Beau Kirsty, and her son Logan, and Hayley's daughter Megan Eve. The first time I held Beau Kirsty was on a Mother's Day, which was strange because the last time I held my Kirsty was on a Mother's Day.

I want with all my heart to leave South Wales and move back to the Midlands to be closer to Sonya and the family, but I have to stay here to be near to Kirsty's grave. She could never bear to be alone and I can't bear to leave her alone; Dave and I bought a plot big enough for us to join Kirsty when the time comes, and Hayley's ashes are coming in my coffin with me. One day we will all be together again.

My heart is crushed, my soul destroyed, and all because of one vile person's terrible actions. But the memories of my two beautiful precious girls are locked up in a golden box within my heart forever. Never again will anyone hurt them, they are safe now, in the arms of the angels.

To lose one child is devastating, but there are no words to describe the pain of losing two. My poor babies are gone, never again will I see them or hold them, not until it is my time to depart this painful world, and I hope that will be soon. Only then will my anguish and pain be over so that I can be reunited with my two beautiful girls forever. On the days that Kirsty and Hayley died, two golden hearts stopped beating.